non

D1414174

781-956-4670 —Tom Dunn

THE ESSENTIAL GUIDE TO
CORPORATE
REAL ESTATE

CoreNet Global, Inc.
Atlanta, Georgia
2015

CoreNet Global
133 Peachtree Street NE, Suite 3000
Atlanta, GA 30303

www.corenetglobal.org

Hardcover: 978-1-932935-004

ePUB: 978-1-932935-02-8

ePDF: 978-1-932935-03-5

Cover design: DiNatale Design, www.dinataledesign.com

Interior Design: Höhne-Werner Design, www.heyneon.com

Table of Contents

Acknowledgements

This book is the culmination of an effort by CoreNet Global and its membership to consolidate our joint expertise and describe the principles governing the practice of corporate real estate. Without the effort of the individuals and organizations below, this book could not have been completed. These CoreNet Global members have devoted their time and their passion to this project by reviewing the content of each chapter. Many have even engaged colleagues, and we thank the individuals, their organizations, and everyone from their organizations who gave freely of their time and expertise.

In 2014, CoreNet Global hired professional writers and provided them with primary source material from the Knowledge Center, the Master of Corporate Real Estate (MCR) Program, the Senior Leader of Corporate Real Estate (SLCR) Program, and the Core Fundamentals Program. These writers created initial drafts to be reviewed by subject matter experts drawn from the association's membership.

Members were invited to submit applications to become one of a limited number of Subject Matter Expert Reviewers. A special task force of the CoreNet Global Board of Directors selected individuals to review each of the book's 17 topical chapters for overall subject matter accuracy and relevance. The final version of this book was the culmination of the input, insights, and expertise from a diverse mix of practitioners from around the world.

We wish to thank and acknowledge a team of dedicated writers who worked through multiple drafts to create *The Essential Guide to Corporate Real Estate:* Molly Badgett, Peter Bowerman, Barbara Horwitz-Bennett, Beth Mattson-Teig, Keith Pierce, Sarah Todd, and Mindi Zissman. We also thank the CoreNet Global staff, including most notably Larry Bazrod, Tim Venable, Amy Dreher and John Gilleard, who were instrumental in bringing this complex project to fruition.

Name	Company
Todd Anderson, MCR, SLCR	Newmark Grubb Knight Frank
Heidi Anderson-Rhodes	DTZ
Monique Arkesteijn	Delft University of Technology
Anoma Baste	Space Matrix Design Consultants Pte Ltd
Kendall Bateman, MCR	T-Mobile
Thomas Bogle	
James Breen	Johnson & Johnson
Tracy Brower, MCR	Mars Drinks
Michael Casolo, MCR	DTZ
David Chang	HSBC
John Coluni	Kaplan
Michael Daly	Time Warner Cable
Michael Davidson	JPMorgan Chase
Helen Desjardins	Sun Life Financial
Dennis Donovan	WDG Consulting
Martin Ecknig	Siemens Ltd., China Shanghai Branch
Robin Ellerthorpe, FAIA	Computerized Facility Integration, LLC CFI
Kelly Ennis	The Verve Partnership
Ty Fastovsky	Trascent Management Consulting, LLC
Iain Franklin	EY
Mark Gorman, MCR, SLCR	Ciena Corporation
Joseph Havey, LEED AP	E Cube, Inc.
Jeff Hayhurst, MCR	State Street Corporation
Christopher Heywood	University of Melbourne
Jennifer Hill	Chevron USA, Inc.
Sophie Hodges	Unilever
Linda Jansen	Lending Club
Ronen Journo, MCR	Cisco
Jamie Kinch	Sonos
Anthony Korvessis, MCR, SLCR	Procter & Gamble
Dominic Lampe, MCR	Raytheon
Susan Lim	Hassell Design (Singapore) Pte Ltd
Peter Lu, MCR	

Name	Company
Carlindo Macedo	HSBC
George McKay	Colliers International
Trevor Miles	IBM Business Consulting
Shaundy Muchin	T-Mobile
Wayne Mullett	Public Works and Government Services Canada
Danielle Myers	
Arnald Ng, MCR	The Hong Kong Jockey Club
Phillip Nye	Cushman & Wakefield
Kurt Ochalla, SLCR, MCR	Philips
Tatsuo Oi, MCR	Wakayama University
Nancy Sanquist	Trimble
Greg Schementi	DTZ
Glen Shenkin, MCR	JLL
Shamsher Sindhu, MCR	Kotak Mahindra Bank Ltd
Matthew Toner	CBRE
Evan Tyroler	DTZ
Peter Van Emburgh, MCR	CBRE
Helmut Weih, MCR	CBRE
Karen Whiteknact	Liberty Mutual Group
Andrea Wolf-Strike, MCR.w	Gensler
Mike Zamora, MCR, SLCR	Asia Real Estate Advisors

Foreword

"I want to be a corporate real estate executive when I grow up." It is unlikely these words were ever uttered by anyone working in this often overlooked and misunderstood profession that's been around since the 1960s.

A career in corporate real estate seems to happen to a person. It's a profession stumbled upon by graduates of all academic disciplines, often years into their working lives. And yet, there are thousands of corporate real estate professionals employed around the world. Doing what exactly?

Ask just about any corporate real estate executive and she'll tell you that her coworkers, friends, and family still aren't sure. "Now what is it that you do again?" asks Great Aunt Edna at every family reunion. "Oh, so you're in commercial real estate? Are you a broker? An investor? Could you help me sell my house?"

That lack of understanding of what corporate real estate is—and what a corporate real estate executive does—led us to create this book.

Designed to be the essential guide for the successful practice of corporate real estate, the pages contained herein were developed with input from leading practitioners and subject matter experts from the CoreNet Global membership base.

This foundational guide was published with multiple audiences in mind:

- Professionals new to corporate real estate roles

- Young leaders growing their skills and understanding of the profession

- Seasoned practitioners deepening their understanding of a specific aspect of their diverse roles

- Colleagues and coworkers in other business units or support functions

- College students exploring a potential career path

- University faculty and academic institutions seeking a resource for introductory corporate real estate content and curriculum development

The guide is divided into 17 chapters, and each highlights the essentials of a key aspect of corporate real estate. Each chapter is introductory in nature and provides only a cursory level of understanding of a complex profession.

This publication defines, acknowledges, and validates a profession that deserves its own guidebook, its own career compass aimed at advancing the practice of corporate real estate.

Angela Cain
Chief Executive Officer
CoreNet Global

CoreNet Global is the internationally recognized association for corporate real estate professionals. The not-for-profit organization provides professional training and development for almost 10,000 members with strategic responsibility for the real estate portfolios of corporations around the world.

Chapter 1

Corporate Real Estate: What Is It All About?

Summary

This chapter provides an introduction to the corporate real estate profession. It is divided into three sections, with the first section offering a definition and overview of corporate real estate and highlighting how the traditional role of corporate real estate is changing. Section two discusses the structure of corporate real estate within organizations, and section three discusses the corporate real estate profession.

Defining Corporate Real Estate

Corporate real estate is a dynamic profession with a broad scope; it touches a wide range of property types, and many functions and careers fall under its umbrella. So, what is corporate real estate? Simply put, it is the real estate necessary to conduct business—the bricks and mortar of office buildings, manufacturing plants and distribution centers, retail stores, and similar facilities. It can include owned or leased space, buildings, and infrastructure, such as power plants or even airport runways.

Defined more technically, corporate real estate refers to the real properties that house the productive or business activities of an organization that owns or leases and, consequently, manages real estate incidental to its primary business objectives, which are *not* real estate. Herein lies an important distinction between corporate and commercial real estate. Although these are two closely related sectors and some real estate professionals may cross over between the two, there is a distinct difference in business objectives. In the commercial real estate world, the business *is* the real estate. The goal for commercial real estate is to provide a risk-adjusted return to the investor; whereas, in corporate real estate, the real estate *supports* the business function. In other words, corporate real estate represents the demand side or user side of real estate, while commercial real estate focuses on the supply side to meet that need.

To better understand the scope and challenge of corporate real estate and its management, it is necessary to consider the five roles of corporate real estate that have been identified over the years in research of this area:

- A strategic resource

- A corporate investment

- A corporate asset

- A commodity that is tradable and may be developed or redeveloped

- Public infrastructure—either as public and not-for-profit corporate real estate, or as contributing to the development of the public realm[1]

Historically, corporate real estate has focused on managing the physical property for the business. Real estate professionals were charged with the basic tasks of acquiring, maintaining, and disposing of real estate throughout the "life cycle" or useful life of a facility. These functions still remain at the core of managing corporate real estate. However, the business landscape has changed, and the role of corporate real estate has also changed, and it continues to evolve. Corporate real estate isn't just about managing facilities and taking orders from the business. It is now about partnering with the business and adding strategic value by contributing to workplace solutions, using real estate space more efficiently, and making recommendations to improve supply chain efficiency. Ultimately, today's corporate real estate leaders are helping to change the conversation from that of real estate as a cost center to one where the role of real estate is to drive value for an organization.

Some view this evolution to mean that corporate real estate today is less about "bricks and mortar" real estate and more about the process of enabling work and helping a business be more productive and competitive in the global economy. The growth in alternative workplace strategies, such as hoteling, desk sharing, and remote working options, demonstrates how corporate real estate is dynamically changing and adapting to new trends in the workplace and the economy.

Organizational Structure

Today's corporate real estate professionals are being challenged to support a variety of corporate initiatives, such as global expansion or contraction, sustainability, competition for talent, speed to market, cost reduction, and improving operational efficiency.[2] Real estate departments are under more pressure to put together a stronger, more efficient, and more effective team of both internal and external resources or partners to accomplish those goals. A number of factors are driving that shift, including:

- Macroeconomic conditions

- Globalization

- Technology

- Demographics

- Sustainability

- Corporate social responsibility

- Realization that corporate real estate can play a bigger strategic role for organizations

One of the notable impacts of the evolution of corporate real estate is that the profession is increasingly viewed as a business discipline, as much as—and possibly even more than—it is seen as a real estate discipline. The business nature of corporate real estate is shifting away from reactive, cost-focused real estate toward a strategic contributor to the business. That shift is most apparent in how corporate real estate is being structured within organizations, most notably with a more direct reporting line to the C-suite or senior corporate leaders such as the chief executive officer, chief finance officer, and chief operating officer.

This section will summarize the organizational structure for corporate real estate as it relates to three separate dimensions:

- The corporate real estate function within the organization

- The corporate real estate function as its own operating unit

- Resourcing the corporate real estate function (in-house sourcing and/or outsourcing)

Corporate Real Estate Function Within the Organization

There is no "one-size-fits all" as it relates to structuring corporate real estate within an organization. In some cases, the corporate real estate manager or department head reports to a company's chief financial officer as real estate can have a significant impact on corporate finances. In other cases, corporate real estate may operate as a support department and report directly to business unit heads with a more client services approach.

In its white paper *Better by Design: Reshaping the CRE Function for Greater Impact,* global real estate services company JLL outlines four basic corporate real estate organizational models.[2] Many companies select one of the four models described below—functional, geographic, process, customer—or opt to create a hybrid matrix or combination of different approaches to best meet their needs. Like the business model, the corporate real estate organizational model is not static but responds and changes along with the needs of the business.

Functional. This traditional corporate real estate model promotes autonomy based on real estate function with each function or "silo" reporting up to the global lead. Examples of those functions would be facilities management, transactions, and construction.

Geographic model. This model allows the global lead to have overall control of the real estate functions with regional executives overseeing local business units and local service providers. For example, a regional head of corporate real estate in China will likely report to the corporate real estate head of Asia Pacific, who in turn reports directly to an organization's global head of corporate real estate.

Process. This model involves structuring the real estate team and its functions around the process of real estate service delivery. Essentially, this model involves matching each activity, such as development, ongoing management or disposition of a property, to the life cycle of real estate.

Customer. A customer model assigns relationship managers to manage business demand from a particular business unit, while portfolio managers and subject matter experts manage the supply side. Relationship managers coordinate a range of strategic and tactical services on behalf of their "customer" or business unit.

A variety of factors go into shaping corporate real estate structure for each individual company, including:

- The corporation's chosen business model, including its leadership and operating philosophy;

- The corporation's position in the industry (i.e., market leader, market laggard);

- The corporation's life cycle (early, high growth, mature, or declining stage); and

- The size and complexity of the real estate portfolio, the number of business operating units, and the frequency with which corporate real estate interacts with executive leaders.

Corporate Real Estate Function As Its Own Operating Unit

Often, the corporate real estate department acts much like its own small business operating within a larger enterprise. Today, experts frequently highlight the importance of aligning corporate real estate strategy with business strategy. As the central point in the real estate planning process, the corporate real estate function is positioned to understand both corporate and business unit perspectives. Real estate works across the entire organization, including the main business units and the various support groups, to ensure that multiple interests are aligned and to optimize cost savings. As such, it is essential for corporate real estate professionals to build relationships with other business units, such as human resources, IT, and operations. Corporate real estate is considered the glue that helps bond the business units.

Although real estate departments are often unique in their structures, they typically share a common objective. The end goal is to organize resources to best manage the real estate facilities, support business critical functions, and support the overall business strategy. Clearly, corporate real estate professionals are adapting to many changes brought on by the competitive business landscape and the ever-evolving corporate real estate environment. One of those changes is that businesses are increasingly using both centralization and outsourcing to "right size" real estate resources and staffing.

Resourcing the Corporate Real Estate Function

The current trend is toward smaller internal corporate real estate teams that engage at a higher level within their own organizations. The question for many firms is how to effectively adapt or change their organizational structures to meet those demands. Some in the profession believe that real estate teams will continue to shrink and centralize, which will require more skills in management, finance, communications, and client relationship management.[3] This minimization of the internal corporate real estate team requires that the real estate consultants and service providers evolve from tactical roles to more strategic partners who anticipate the needs of their corporate real estate clients. That shift also means more attention must be paid to better managing both internal and external resources.

As corporate real estate organizations change from tactical to strategic orientations, service provider relationships are evolving to the partnership level in many companies.[4] A cooperative working relationship between these partners is a critical component in maintaining the right balance between in-house and outsourced services. Since corporate real estate organizations are facing diverse needs, many are utilizing an outsourcing model. The size of an internal real estate department or the extent of the external, outsourced real estate resources can depend on many factors, including the size and geographic footprint of an organization's real estate portfolio and its business philosophy.

Real Estate Functions

Functional real estate skills can be utilized in many different areas throughout the life cycle of a facility, such as handling transactions, managing facilities, administering leases, and overseeing and controlling construction projects. Each of those areas has its own layers of additional tasks and duties. Transactions, for example, can relate to the purchase, sale or lease of property. Facilities management includes numerous responsibilities, ranging from overseeing equipment maintenance and cleaning to energy management and catering and hospitality.

To that end, the broad corporate real estate profession includes a variety of different careers, functions, and specialties in areas such as design, finance, construction, business development, engineering, brokerage, facilities and property management, workplace strategy, client relationship management, change management, and sustainability. Many corporate real estate professionals have a property-related background such as architecture, construction, property management, real estate transactions, finance, or accounting. However, there are many different entry points and career opportunities within corporate real estate. The profession offers a wide variety of jobs, including project manager, real estate transactions specialist, facility manager, financial analyst, client relationship manager, and director of real estate—to name only a few.

People tend to begin their real estate careers in an area of specialization. However, it is important to understand the bigger picture of available career opportunities. For example, an individual might start out working as a facility manager and move into other roles as his or her career matures and knowledge of the industry grows. That facility manager might eventually become an asset manager, sales associate, or head of real estate services.

The evolving role of corporate real estate also is reflected in the desirable skill set that corporate real estate professionals possess today. CoreNet Global research has indicated that employers are increasingly focusing on core competencies and character traits as much as substantive skills when they are hiring corporate real estate executives.[5] Employers want individuals who have excellent communication and interpersonal skills. Due to the changing business environment, employers also see the need for general business acumen in areas such as change management, performance management, and the ability to define enterprise alignment. Specifically, corporations are looking to staff or support corporate real estate positions with generalists who can subsequently develop the necessary functional competency or skills specific to real estate. Many programs focus on general real estate or areas tangential to real estate. Because of this "skills gap," knowledge and skills are often learned on the job or through established industry programs such as the CoreNet Global Master of Corporate Real Estate (MCR) and Senior Leader of Corporate Real Estate (SLCR) programs.

Research also has shown that corporate executives perceive a gap between what skills are essential for success and the current capabilities of their teams.[4] In order to enhance their skill set, corporate real estate professionals need to define the core purpose and deliverables they need to bring to their business units. Another alternative for organizations is to leverage partnerships and outsourcing to fill those performance gaps. Such partnerships already play an increasingly important role in creating efficiencies and driving value to the organization, and it is likely that these will become even more important in the future.

The Corporate Real Estate Profession

The corporate real estate profession consists of all the individuals employed in real estate management by end-user companies and those employed by the many supplier companies who provide real estate services to those end-user clients: construction firms, real estate service providers, consultants, attorneys, brokers, architects, technology vendors, economic developers and many others. Together, these comprise the entire corporate real estate supply chain, or ecosystem.

That corporate real estate ecosystem is large, global, and diverse. As such, it affords abundant opportunities for a wide range of individuals with varying skills and backgrounds and at different stages of their careers.

The supply side of the corporate real estate profession is larger in terms of overall employment than the end-user or demand side. As a result, it offers a wide range of opportunities, and younger professionals in particular often work for a real estate services company.[6]

The demand side of corporate real estate also offers great career opportunities. Individuals employed by large multinational corporations find the work challenging and rewarding. Salaries are competitive and on the rise, reflecting the growing importance of corporate real estate management and its ability to add business value.

For example, the 2014 CoreNet Global End User Compensation survey, conducted in collaboration with Chicago-based FPL Associates L.P., revealed that average total annual compensation, including salary, cash bonus and long-term incentive, reached $277,391 USD for senior end users with global responsibility (e.g., the top end user in the corporate real estate organization). For those in the 75th percentile, the figure was $336,980 USD.[7]

Conclusion

Corporate real estate is a dynamic profession with a broad scope; it touches a wide range of property types, and many functions and careers fall under its umbrella. Distinct from commercial real estate, corporate real estate is the real estate necessary to conduct business – to support the business function.

Today's corporate real estate leaders are helping to change the conversation from that of real estate as a cost center to one where the role of real estate is to drive value for an organization. One of the notable impacts of the evolution of corporate real estate is that the profession is increasingly viewed as a business discipline, as much as—and possibly even more than—it is seen as a real estate discipline.

References

1. Heywood, C., & Kenley, R. (2013). *Five axioms for corporate real estate management: A polemical review of the literature.* Paper presented at the Nineteenth Pacific Rim Real Estate Society Conference, Melbourne, Australia. Available from http://www.prres. net/

2. Bayne-Jardine, T., Frost, S., Schuth, J., & Carroll, T. (2011, April). *Better by design: Reshaping the CRE function for greater impact.* JLL Retrieved from: https://resources.corenetglobal.org/knowledgecenteronline/SearchByTopicAndResource.aspx?ID=4252

3. Evans, B. (2012, March/April). A recipe for success: The globalization of real estate management structures. *The LEADER.* Retrieved from https://resources.corenetglobal.org/knowledgecenteronline/SearchByTopicAndResource.aspx?ID=5978

4. Anderson, M., & Levine, D. (2009, September). The evolution of corporate real estate: Up-skilling the downsized CRE organization. *CoreNet Global.* Retrieved from https://resources.corenetglobal.org/knowledgecenteronline/SearchByTopicAndResource.aspx?ID=4383

5. Kamath, N. and Horton, I. (2012, November/December). "Upskilling" the organization advances relationship building, cross-functional collaboration and change management. *The LEADER.* Retrieved from https://resources.corenetglobal.org/knowledgecenteronline/SearchByTopicAndResource.aspx?ID=1668

6. CoreNet Global. (2015, July/August). 36 under 36: CoreNet Global's up-and-coming young leaders. *The LEADER.* Retrieved from https://resources.corenetglobal.org/knowledgecenteronline/SearchByTopicAndResource.aspx?ID=7259

7. CoreNet Global and FPL Associates L.P. (2015, January). 2014 CoreNet Global End User Compensation Survey. Retrieved from https://resources.corenetglobal.org/knowledgecenteronline/SearchByTopicAndResource.aspx?ID=7035

Chapter 2

Location and Site Selection

Summary

The purpose of this chapter is to help corporate real estate professionals better understand the numerous factors that influence site selection and location decisions for organizations. It also will provide some resources and guidelines to help corporate real estate professionals navigate the often highly complex site selection process.

It is divided into three sections, with section one examining how the real estate footprint and workplace is evolving and highlighting some of the key influences on how and where people work today. Section two explores how factors such as the economy, globalization, and technology are driving change to the corporate real estate portfolio because every organization has its own unique location needs and priorities. Section three offers insights on how professionals can gain a better understanding of those needs and ultimately how they can make decisions that help drive value for their organizations.

The Corporate Footprint: Land, Buildings, and Workplace

The main role of the corporate real estate team is to support the corporation's key objectives, business plans, and metrics by providing adequate facilities in the appropriate locations. Fundamentally, that means finding the right amount of space in the right location, at the right time, and often at the right price. From a location perspective, that all boils down to one simple question—where? Where to locate new facilities, where to close underutilized properties, and where to consolidate operations?

Location decisions today are affected by numerous external trends such as technology, changing demographics, urbanization, globalization, and the development of emerging markets—not to mention the changing demands occurring within organizations. This section aims to highlight some of the key trends shaping location decisions for today's corporate real estate professionals.

Technology and Innovation

Technology is changing the way companies work and how organizations structure their workspace. Yet even though the "virtual office" and an increasingly mobile workforce will continue to impact where and how work is done, it has not lessened the value of the physical workplace. The brick-and-mortar location is still an important part of business operations as workers come together to collaborate, innovate, and enhance productivity. Furthermore, real estate is a concrete part of an organization's values and image it is striving to create.

That being said, technology is impacting space utilization and how the physical space is structured. Mobile devices mean workers no longer have to remain stationary, and today's workers are often proficient working from any place and at any time. That shift is impacting the size and design of the corporate office. Overall, there is a broader trend among corporations to use real estate more efficiently, requiring less space per employee. Changing work styles are also prompting companies to create more open, collaborative workspaces, which are increasingly replacing cubicle and personal office-based designs.

For geographic deployment of business operations, real time data has become indispensable in maximizing the value of the corporate real estate footprint. In particular, there has been an emergence of:

- Dashboards, utilizing business intelligence tools that go beyond static information allowing for trend analysis, forecasting, and drill-down capabilities;

- The cloud, which helps put a complex of networks on the same page; and

• Integration of HR and real estate data to better understand the capability of existing operations to accommodate selected types of growth.

Modern building management equipment provides a remote, 24/7 information fountain, which is another kind of big data.

Millennials

It is critical for location strategies to reflect the dynamic shift of millennials in the workforce. Millennials, also known as Generation Y, represent a growing percentage of the workforce and are expected to account for the majority of new hires occurring within the next decade. Although the definition varies, millennials are generally viewed as individuals born between 1977 and 1995. In the U.S. alone, the millennial generation is expected to reach 75.3 million in 2015, exceeding that of the baby boomer population (1946–1964) at 74.9 million for the first time, according to data from the Pew Research Center.[1]

As firms compete for available talent, employers cannot ignore the needs, desires, and attitudes of this generation. Millennials are the most highly educated generation in history, and they have their own views on work / life balance. In the workplace, millennials gravitate toward teamwork, collaboration, and technology, although—like any group—this generation also has its share of introverts who like their private space.

Millennials prefer to rent housing rather than buy. In addition, many millennials weathered the "Great Recession" by accepting jobs that were not in line with their original career goals and that paid lower wages relative to their education and experience.[2] What this means is that millennials are more mobile and not tied to one place or one job. According to one 2014 survey, 90 percent of millennials do *not* plan to stay with an employer longer than five years; 37 percent plan to stay no more than two years, and 40% starting a new job are already considering their next move.[3]

How and where millennials work is forcing companies to rethink how space is configured and where those offices are located. In the U.S., for example, millennials have been leading a broader shift in urbanization as they look to live, work, and play in core cities. Even when settling down and starting a family, they prefer homes in walkable inner-ring suburbs rather than auto-dominant exurbs. It is important to locate facilities near that young labor pool, as well as select locations that have adequate parking and access to mass transit. In addition, companies need to offer collaborative and updated workspace with amenities that appeal to millennials. Ultimately, that extra attention to the details and many factors that influence millennial workers will yield long-term benefits by helping to reduce costs and inefficiencies associated with employee turnover.

Onshoring and Near-Shoring

Corporations are increasingly looking to adjust supply chains as they adapt to a changing global environment. Companies are debating the pros and cons of offshoring, reshoring, or near-shoring manufacturing plants, and business processing or back-office operations and the associated localization strategies. Finding the right solution depends heavily on the unique dynamics of an organization and product, as well as key factors such as production costs, manufacturing processes, and proximity to a customer base.[4]

Manufacturers are beginning to recognize that many of the variables that go into location analysis, such as transportation and labor costs, have changed dramatically in recent years. The clear cost advantages in countries such as China have been diminishing amid higher transportation costs and rising wages. The declining cost advantages for offshoring, along with dynamics such as higher productivity in developed nations, are some of the factors behind the shift to "reshore" or "near-shore" manufacturing to lower cost markets closer to home.

Yet, at the same time, those global location decisions are not always driven solely by cost. Organizations ranging from manufacturers to service-sector companies are expanding global footprints to penetrate new markets. China, for example, first emerged as a location target for multinational corporations because of its reputation as a low-cost producer of goods. However, China's rapidly growing middle class has already well exceeded that of the total population of the U.S. and is projected to reach 630 million by 2022, according to market data from McKinsey & Company. For many reasons, it may be desirable to participate from within a market instead of solely shipping all product, service, and competences into it.

In the service sector, which includes customer service centers, shared services centers, transaction processing operations, and IT centers, many corporations adopt a "follow the sun" deployment strategy. The global footprint will be geographically balanced to reflect dynamics such as time zone, labor supply / cost, language capabilities, labor market regulation and flexibility, accessibility, risk, and security. Flexibility to upsize or downsize the footprint based on market conditions must be woven into the geographic deployment strategy of companies' location decisions.

Managing Real Estate Portfolios

Drivers for location decisions are clearly changing. This means that corporate real estate professionals are increasingly being called upon to manage risks, utilize space efficiently, and incorporate more flexibility into a portfolio to account for market or operational changes.

Flexibility. One of the recurring themes for corporate real estate executives across property types—from manufacturing plants to corporate headquarters—is the need for flexibility that will allow companies to adjust the global or regional footprint as business conditions warrant. Flexibility can pertain to a variety of aspects of managing a portfolio, including financing, workspace design, and corporate real estate's own organization structure.[5]

Some view leasing instead of owning real estate as one way to achieve greater flexibility. For example, leases can create added flexibility by adding terms that allow organizations to expand or contract as business conditions change. Terms and options such as a right of first refusal can give a tenant the right to lease additional space. Tenants also can secure rights to sublease excess space that may become available during the course of their lease.

Additionally, flexibility of the physical workplace must be imbued in facility design, such as modular or multipurpose work spaces. Organizational flexibility often refers to how work is distributed within an organization, such as outsourcing or working with strategic partners. The term also might apply to workplace strategies, such as remote or telework situations. The same amount of attention has to be paid to factory design, and whether it is advisable to design the space so it could accommodate a future shift in use, such as a shift in all or part of production space to warehouse or training.

Shrinking footprint. Technology, changing work styles, and a focus on "rightsizing" real estate all contribute to the shrinking corporate real estate footprint. The global financial crisis created even more pressure for organizations to cut costs and improve efficiencies. Firms need to do more with less, including real estate, which can represent the second- or third-largest operating expense for some organizations. Some view this next evolutional step as a looming "Industry 4.0," a term that refers to the "fourth industrial revolution" or the use of electronics and IT to further automate production. Similar to other industrial revolutions in history, Industry 4.0 could lead to another huge leap forward in increasing business productivity. It would also have a significant impact on the logistics of corporate real estate in terms of how much space is needed, how it is configured, and where it is located.

The cumulative effect of many of these factors is a contracting real estate footprint per capita for many organizations.

Rebalancing the supply chain. Multinational corporations are working to achieve a better geographic balance in the global real estate footprint. That balance is particularly important as companies seek to minimize the costs and risks of long, complicated supply chains and locate production and service facilities closer to customer demand. According to the CoreNet Global Corporate Real Estate 2020 End-User Survey, 68 percent of respondents agreed that business continuity and supply chain logistics will be critical factors in location strategies. As companies continue to balance supply chains, priorities in determining the best location choices may include the ones below:

- Adequate infrastructure will be important for all sectors, especially manufacturing, distribution, and research and development.

- Supply chain cost / risk will be overriding concerns for manufacturing and distribution.

- Customer access / service delivery times will be key for distribution and a significant proportion of manufacturing industries.

- Presence of other similar companies and support networks will be a prime location determinant for a number of manufacturing sectors, such as biotech, aerospace, and nearly all research and development.[6]

Long, extended global supply chains have become risky, costly, and somewhat inflexible. Consequently, there is a notable trend toward interconnected, regional strategies that are often called a multi-local supply chain strategy. This strategy aims to balance the advantages of global economies of scale with local service and responsiveness.[6] As companies learn from each other, as well as from leaders in their respective industries, more regional production facilities are likely in the years ahead.

Site Selection Criteria and Process

Numerous factors weigh heavily in the site selection process, including those related to key categories such as business costs, logistics, risks, infrastructure, and labor supply to name a few. Ultimately, location strategy needs to help align the real estate portfolio with business strategy, which is a key theme in corporate real estate.

According to a 2012 CoreNet Global Location Strategy Survey, 79 percent of respondents said they clearly link location strategy to the company's business drivers and operating strategies, such as finding talent, entering new markets, supply chain efficiency, and tax minimization. The real challenge for corporate real estate professionals is to continue to adapt and improve that process in an ever-changing landscape.

It is important to note that the value of different site selection criteria can vary depending on the organization and the industry. For instance, within the business process outsourcing sector (e.g., IT, call center, back office), it is all about labor supply, quality, cost. In manufacturing and distribution, logistics are often paramount. But once a geographic region is chosen based on logistics, labor will once again assume the primary position as a site selection factor. For research and development, access to talent is critical, as is local knowledge acquisition and links to universities and other industry resources. For corporate headquarters, global air service, support services, and executive / professional talent are overriding factors. In retail, demographics within reasonable proximity to a site are overarching. This requires micro-geographic analysis (e.g., zip code or census block) to help quantify market opportunities.

Understanding the unique needs, priorities, and business structure of an individual organization—or even the individual unit within one organization—becomes the most important dynamic. Company size and growth strategy also can influence location decisions. For most companies, labor—costs, skills, and availability—has traditionally been a key driver in location decisions. As technology and connectivity continue to play a crucial role in business operations, any search for offshore locations may need to prioritize IT functionality and IT-enabled services. Corporate real estate professionals also need to consider the re-use, sub-lease or disposal likelihood of a facility. That is why it is critical to develop location strategy with input from many different stakeholders within an organization, such as human resources, IT, finance, legal, security, the C-Suite, and division heads from specific regions or business units.

Access to labor. Access to both talent and labor at reasonable costs are primary site selection criteria for most organizations and functions. Access to talent has certainly fostered key industry clusters, such as Silicon Valley for technology and Boston for life sciences. Specific to workforce availability, it is important to understand how the labor market in a country or even a particular region or city functions. Corporate real estate professionals need to work closely with human resource professionals to not only understand the company's labor needs, but also to develop a hiring strategy specific to that country or location. When selecting a location or combination of locations for operations, companies should prioritize their labor and talent considerations and define minimum / maximum requirements.[8]

When selecting a site or building within a metro area, the concept of labor submarkets must be applied. The targeted site / building should confer a labor market advantage for the business in question. Specifically, the property should be readily accessible to primary labor pools. Ideally, the site will allow a company to enjoy a competitive edge in workforce recruitment and retention. When deciding on a final site, the "best real estate deal" may also need to be a good "HR deal."

Labor costs—wages, benefits, and other compensation—are paramount when weighing the economics of location options. For example, companies locating a call center in an area where agents speak English plus one other European language will find that labor costs associated with locating in a major European city such as London or Frankfurt can be more than double the cost of locating in an offshore Asia city such as Mumbai or nearshore Africa such as Casablanca.[4] For some European companies, those higher costs are prompting organizations to consider other "off-shore" or "near-shore" options in areas of northern Africa that have lower wages and good language skills.

Incentives. Government incentives can play a major role in location decisions, in choosing both where to locate in a specific country and where to locate at the region, state, provincial, or city level. Incentives can take many different shapes and forms from offers of free land and tax rebates to assistance in locating and training key labor and expedited construction permitting. In the U.S. alone, an estimated $8 billion in economic incentives were offered in 2014 to attract various corporate expansion projects—ranging from corporate headquarters to manufacturing plants—according to estimates from the Site Selection Group.[9] The largest economic incentive deal in 2014 was a $1.3 billion package offered to Tesla Motors to build the world's largest lithium-ion battery plant in Reno, Nevada.

Location Scorecard and Financial Option Comparison

Once a location strategy framework is in place, many site selection experts develop their own steps and systematic processes to aid in geographic deployment decisions. For example, some professionals utilize a "location scorecard" to help compare and contrast different location options. Creating a location scorecard or weighted rating scale can be a helpful tool for prioritizing site selection criteria and evaluating location alternatives.

Rating models typically use a point system to rank locations based on a scale—such as a '0' for *least favorable* and '9' for *most favorable*. Typically, there will be two scorecards, one for qualitative considerations (e.g., labor market) and the other for costs. The best locations will be those scoring highest on operational or qualitative concerns and lowest on cost variables—or a reasonable balance between the two.

Conclusion

Decisions about location and site selection involve a comprehensive strategic planning process that requires ample time to prepare. Added to that is the dual challenge of meeting business demands to improve efficiencies and reduce costs while still accommodating future growth and remaining flexible to adapt to changes within the organization or within competitive markets.

Corporate real estate professionals can equip themselves to better meet those challenges. Some of the fundamentals to success in site selection and location decisions include having a keen understanding of which criteria are most important to your organization. Professionals must make sure that location strategy aligns with business strategy and that key stakeholders are involved in the process. Maximum flexibility will be important for property types from manufacturing plants to corporate headquarters, as flexibility will allow companies to adapt as needs change, use space more efficiently, and reduce the risk of financial burden from outdated, underutilized properties. A structured process can help to identify and evaluate locations.

References

1. Fry, R. (2015). This year, Millennials will overtake Baby Boomers. *Pew Research Center.* Retrieved from http://www.pewresearch.org/fact-tank/2015/01/16/this-year-millennials-will-overtake-baby-boomers/

2. U.S. Chamber of Commerce Foundation. (2012). *The Millennial generation research review.* Retrieved from http://www.uschamberfoundation.org/millennial-generation-research-review

3. Kingl, A., & Hytner, R. (2014). *Generation Y paradigms of work and leadership.* London Business School, Deloitte Consulting. Retrieved from http://www.slideshare.net/londonbusinessschool/gls-adamkingl

4. Buck, R., Brammer, A., van der Hout, D., & van Aalst, W. (2012). *Location, location, location: How global real estate strategy leads to corporate success.* CoreNet Global EMEA Summit, Amsterdam. Retrieved from https://resources.corenetglobal.org/knowledgecenteronline/SearchByTopicAndResource.aspx?ID=1250

5. Apgar, M. (2009, Nov. 30). What every leader should know about real estate. *Harvard Business Review.*

6. Mattson-Teig, B. (2012, May). *Corporate real estate 2020 final report: Location strategy and the role of place.* CoreNet Global. Retrieved from: https://resources.corenetglobal.org/knowledgecenteronline/SearchByTopicAndResource.aspx?ID=2052

7. DHL. (2013, Jan. 6.) *The rise of local.* Retrieved from http://www.supplychaindigital.com/procurement/2131/A-localised-supply-chain-could-minimise-disaster-risk.

8. Jackson, M. (n.d.). *How to evaluate offshore locations for IT-enabled services.* JLL.

9. Rendziperis, K. (2015, Jan. 16). Top 10 economic incentive deals of 2014. Site Selection Group Blog. http://info.siteselectiongroup.com/blog/top-10-economic-incentive-deals-2014

Chapter 3

Portfolio Management

Summary

Portfolio management is a relatively recent discipline within corporate real estate. Initially begun in the 1990s within large firms, the principles underlying portfolio management have since been adopted across the profession. The goal of portfolio management is to be more intentional and proactive and to secure a long-term view of a company's real estate assets, given that they typically rank among the top three expenditures of the corporation.

If a firm can manage across locations, departments, and disciplines in a holistic manner (considering the enterprise's space needs as a single portfolio with no silos), then that company can more effectively maximize the productivity of its space, avoid costly mistakes, and enhance flexibility as needs change and adjustments are made for market conditions. Although it is impossible to fully "future-proof" a company's assets, professionals seeking to develop a comprehensive strategy for them can unlock value, achieve cost savings, and gain a seat at the table as the firm's executive leadership plans for the future.

Introduction

For many years, an organization's real estate management was likely to be compartmentalized, whether by business group or region, with space acquired or disposed of based on local needs. While consideration may have been given to the future needs of a local enterprise, little attention was given to whether another group within the organization might benefit from any surplus space. That has changed, and portfolio management is currently considered an essential tool for managing multiple locations and even types of space across a company's real estate holdings based on an analysis of supply and demand trends throughout the enterprise.

This chapter is divided into three parts and introduces the concept of portfolio management and some principles that guide its use in corporate real estate. The first section explains the concept of portfolio management and discusses why it might be beneficial to the enterprise. The second part explains many of the processes most common to portfolio management and provides an overview of its role in the organization. Some challenges to portfolio management that are often encountered by professionals in the field will be examined in the third section, which is followed by a case study / example and some concluding thoughts.

Concept and Principles

Portfolio management was developed in response to increasingly complex corporate real estate needs. While initially driven by a desire to better mitigate risk and avoid unnecessary costs, portfolio management professionals today also strive to enhance the productivity of workers and business units and maintain the most flexibility regarding space needs while maximizing value across the enterprise. Conceptually, portfolio management is exactly what its name implies: the management of a company's real estate portfolio at a macro level instead of looking at each lease or purchase separately based on local demands.

In practice, this carries many complexities, such as considering changes in the industry, weighing long- and short-term space needs against acquisition costs, developing a strategy for disposing of surplus assets, and balancing all variables against ongoing market dynamics. In order to better understand the concept of portfolio management, we should consider five guiding principles of the profession.

1. A Factor of Production

Real estate from an occupier perspective is a cost; although it can generate income under some circumstances, its acquisition usually is necessitated by production, whether that product is a good or a service. Thus, one goal of portfolio management is to have enough of the right space but no more than necessary of any type of space.

2. Duration Matching

As the name implies, the second principle of portfolio management is matching the duration of an investment in space to the expected time it will be needed. Put simply, when managing both space and costs, the necessary question should not be, "Should you own or lease?" but rather, "Will you need this space for a long or a short time?" The answers to this question can then inform issues of lease or ownership. Of course, this principle also involves aligning supply with demand given the uncertainty of changing needs and market dynamics. Depending on market costs and other factors, long-term, stable needs might lead to the ownership of property such as a manufacturing facility.

Short-term needs or those with a degree of uncertainty, such as a seasonal increase in production or an expansion into a new sales region, might suggest the need for leased space or even shared space. The goal underlying this principle is to avoid or minimize risks while exercising sufficient control over properties essential to ongoing operations or for branding purposes. In most cases, real estate transactions are outside of the core competencies of a company.

3. Analysis of Clusters, Not Just Assets

The third and fourth principles are closely related and concern how space is considered and managed within the portfolio. A cluster is any grouping of similar space requirements; they can be aggregated by segment, campus location, market or region, or use. Clustering allows for a higher-level view of real estate rather than considering each asset separately or managing assets simply by business group or division, which may lead to missed opportunities and unnecessary costs. For example, one division may cease to require a distribution warehouse in New Jersey just as another group develops a need for the same kind of space in that location. If the lease has not yet expired, this space is still a potential asset for the second group, which might help the organization avoid the double liability of an existing cost and a new expense.

4. Managing Duration by Cluster or Segment

Again, this principle imparts benefits in both value and flexibility that are less likely to be realized if each asset is considered separately. The duration of investments and the composition and arrangement of clusters and segments should all be reevaluated periodically to ensure that maximum value is being pursued and realized.

5. Financial Underwriting

As noted previously, operational corporate real estate is a cost that requires appropriate financial management. Working outside of one's core competencies increases risk, so this fifth principle requires portfolio management professionals to work in concert with the organization's finance team. It is important to begin with sound financial management practices and then to consider generally accepted accounting principles, international financial reporting standards, and tax implications.

While portfolio management begins with the question, "What assets are needed?" bringing financial considerations into the equation enables the team to answer the follow-up question, "How does the company pay for the assets?" As with the principle of duration matching, long-term structures are most appropriate for stable requirements, while short-term arrangements make more financial sense for more volatile or uncertain requirements, even though this is likely to increase costs during the hold period.

These principles underlie the concept of portfolio management and guide the processes utilized by corporate real estate professionals, which are examined in the next section.

Process and Role

Over time, portfolio management has developed from a series of intuitive theories tested by corporate real estate departments into a more systemic set of practices / processes followed by the majority of professionals in the field. The process of planning for portfolio management can be broken down into seven general steps, which are described below.

1. Understand Business Drivers

This first step involves knowing the factors that affect real estate needs across the enterprise. These factors can run from the most general level—changes within the industry or economy—to specific factors at the company or even business unit level. An understanding of these drivers and which direction they are moving—expansion, diffusion, contraction, or more literal directions such as toward the Middle East or South America—will assist in planning for portfolio management.

2. Understand Existing State of Portfolio

The second step involves aligning corporate real estate with the strategy of the overall enterprise and individual business units. Portfolio management professionals should understand where corporate real estate falls within the organization's planning process, be able to define the impact of the identified drivers on demand within the organization, and be ready to assess how portfolio management strategies can support the core business. This process is highly iterative, as near-constant reappraisal is required in a large organization.

3. Develop a Supply-and-Demand Profile

This step entails understanding the supply of space: the availability, amount, and location of different types of space and the terms for obtaining that space. The same questions apply to the demand for space: what type, how much, where should it be located, and how long will it be needed? While there are many dimensions to this step, its successful completion enables portfolio management to align supply to demand as much as possible.

4. Identify Like-Kind Requirements

The first three steps lay the foundation for the next ones. The fourth step requires an examination of clusters or segments to identify similar needs across different regions or business units.

5. Identify Gaps and Evaluate Options

This step, often referred to as "gap analysis," allows the corporate real estate professional to identify current and potential gaps in the portfolio in a variety of scenarios and explore the most effective ways to resolve those gaps based on the overall enterprise's business strategy. Typically, several options are presented that cover a range of scenarios from conservative to aggressive, with varying financial impacts.

6. Develop Recommendations and Seek Necessary Approvals

This step consolidates the intelligence compiled to this point into a series of recommended actions, which can then be presented to more senior management for approval.

7. Implement and Govern

The final step follows naturally. After a plan is presented based upon the above steps, decisions can be made about which actions to take, how to undertake and manage those actions, and how to periodically evaluate results for value and effectiveness.

The value of this exercise depends to a large degree on the value and integrity of the data gathered. If data is consistent and easily accessible to all parties, then all the variables can be considered and the conclusions can be tested, both initially and over the duration of the commitment. Ranking or weighting different scenarios or considerations can allow a decision matrix to be followed quickly and tested by others, leading to conclusions that are more likely to be data-driven than based on instincts or assumptions.

Challenges

Portfolio management is an art as well as a science, and even the best data lacks the ability to "future-proof" a company's real estate holdings, leading to a number of challenges for professionals in this field.

External Uncertainty

Every portfolio management professional faces external uncertainties as unexpected events are—by their definition—difficult to anticipate. These events can include changes to the external environment, such as regulatory, political, or economic demands, as well as changes to the business, including shifting industry trends, declining product life cycles, or the emergence of new technologies.

Industry Volatility

Most industries lack complete stability. Even mature industries can see changes in competition, distribution channels, or product mix. Shifts in the rate of change can shorten the planning horizon and make it more difficult to project accurately, even with sophisticated scenario modeling.

Different Growth Stages

A variety of growth stages also present challenges to accurate forecasting and modeling. Whether a business or industry is in growth mode, has reached a plateau of maturity, or is repositioning to stave off decline, each stage presents its own challenges to portfolio management. In addition, it is difficult to know when a business is entering a new stage.

Mismatch of Expectations

Two other challenges are less externally focused and closer to the processes of portfolio management. First is the possibility of mismatched expectations. Corporate real estate carries the responsibility of balancing flexibility in the face of change, finding value while obtaining the appropriate facilities, and engaging in both financial and reputational risk. The lowest occupancy costs are generally found in long-term leases or owned properties, but these investments also offer the least flexibility. Maximum flexibility is found in leasing spaces for the shortest lengths of time possible, but these are generally the most expensive arrangements. Lower-quality properties offer lower costs but may negatively impact a brand or workplace productivity if conditions are not appropriate.

Supply-Demand Mismatch

Similar to the mismatch of expectations, a mismatch in supply and demand may also occur. Real estate is by its nature inflexible: a building does not easily change its size and cannot generally be relocated. Additionally, procuring or disposing of space is a slow and costly process. Demand drivers, on the other hand, are often volatile, unexpected, and sudden, as was discussed above. And the more one drills down in location or property type, the more volatile demand becomes, due to the increased difficulty in locating appropriate space.

Although some of these challenges are not easily overcome, they can be considered as corporate real estate professionals work to mitigate risk and retain maximum flexibility. The optimal mix of flexibility, value, and risk is difficult to achieve, but understanding these portfolio challenges and communicating them to company leaders can help to manage expectations as to what "successful" portfolio management might look like.

Case Study

To better understand these principles and processes, consider how they are applied to a specific case that might be encountered by a company's real estate department. In this example, a company is realigning its portfolio following a merger with another organization. In 2009, this company found itself with more than 500 sites in 80 countries, with a number of similar—and therefore overlapping—spaces in metropolitan areas. The challenge was to quickly reduce the new company's more than 100 million-square-foot (9.3 million-square-meter) footprint, and its attendant costs, by consolidating where possible and closing sites that were no longer needed. The corporate real estate team also saw a need to develop an ongoing review process for its holdings. As a result the team created a long-range plan for portfolio management with the following objectives:

- Create a portfolio for the new company with the best combination of size, value, and location to suit the firm's strategic objectives;

- Improve the portfolio's flexibility;

- Improve the transparency of the process;

- Support optimal financial planning;

- Streamline processes and governance for management of the portfolio, so that it aligned with the company's priorities; and

- Reduce portfolio costs by 10% outside the United States.

Additionally, the corporate real estate team was guided by four principles. Their long-range plan was intended to: 1) drive a more progressive use of space, 2) maximize the flexibility of the portfolio, 3) support overall business goals, and 4) push costs and productivity toward maximum efficiency.

The team launched the project with a period of discovery, which included creating the principles outlined above, collecting data on space, interviewing key stakeholders, and developing an understanding of business requirements in the newly merged company. These efforts led into an analysis of the available supply in various markets around the world and of the business units' demands and requirements for space.

At this stage, the company's corporate real estate professionals began to develop alternative plans for meeting demands while keeping both flexibility and financial costs in mind. They applied techniques such as benchmarking against peers, gap analysis, and considering the ideal state of the portfolio, while understanding that the ideal might not be possible. All sites were examined on the basis of cost, efficiency, and suitability to occupant needs. These measurements were benchmarked against company averages and goals, which provided insight into which best matched company goals.

Regions were also scored, with an eye toward determining the cost and value of operating in a particular city or market. For instance, if costs were lower and efficiency greater in Beijing than in Shanghai, the team could better assess the value of focusing more resources in Beijing and fewer in Shanghai. (Of course, the process must take into account other considerations, such as governmental structure and transportation infrastructure, but initial scenarios were based purely on real estate considerations.)

As regional baselines were set, the company's portfolio management team set performance targets, such as the ideal amount of space required per office employee, and assessed the ability of different business groups and locations to make a change. These metrics were scored on a grid to show which locations offered the greatest opportunity to shift into new modes of operating and better align with the previously identified core principles. At this point, the long-range portfolio plan was presented to key executives. Following their endorsement, key regional stakeholders and the facilities management team were engaged in the process. Target sites were then prioritized, and the plan was executed.

Of course, that is not the end of the process. As with any plan, this one needed to be refined as new information was uncovered. Progress was monitored, and feedback was sought from those in the affected locations. Even after the plan's completion, work was needed to institutionalize the changes and continue to communicate the company's values regarding real estate and efficiency. The value, utility, and cost of space will continue to be reassessed periodically to ensure that goals are being reached as market conditions shift.

Conclusion

When properly executed, portfolio management can not only add value but also maximize efficiency and help balance the desire for the most flexibility with the need to minimize risk—financial and otherwise—within the boundaries that the organization sets. These objectives are best accomplished with the cooperation and buy-in of business unit and corporate executives who respect the value of corporate real estate professionals and keep them in "in the loop" regarding corporate strategy and new developments in products or services.

If solutions and scenarios are data-driven and aligned with corporate priorities and other support functions, then a stronger portfolio can be achieved. While the ideal may be unreachable and some factors are difficult to predict, a more effective and efficient portfolio can be attained each time the process is implemented.

Chapter 4

Property Life Cycle

Summary

This chapter looks at the impact of the entire property life cycle—from concept to retirement—on the corporate portfolio. At both the property and portfolio levels, the real estate life cycle generally runs from acquisition through the length of its holding period to the disposition of space at the end of its economic usefulness (including remediation if necessary).

This life cycle must be managed carefully to maximize the value of the portfolio and minimize unnecessary costs. While corporate real estate professionals will be most involved at the beginning and end of the property life cycle, their oversight and analysis can serve the enterprise at all phases. Therefore, it is important that corporate real estate professionals understand each phase and its financial implications.

Managing Property Life Cycle

Managing the property life cycle requires applying the principles and processes of portfolio management, aligning the portfolio with strategic business drivers and priorities while also allowing flexibility to react to external or internal business changes. Data-driven analysis, supply-and-demand dynamics, and periodic reevaluation are important to both portfolio management and the management of the property life cycle. As in portfolio management, change is the norm in the property life cycle. New construction or acquisitions often are underway at the same time that leasehold expansions or extensions are being negotiated and surplus space is being disposed of through subleases or sales.

To ensure that terms are commonly understood, it is important to define *acquisition, holding period,* and *disposition* as they will be used in this chapter. *Acquisition* refers to adding space to the portfolio, which can be accomplished through leasing, purchasing, or building to the company or business unit's demands. Acquisition launches the property's life cycle, from the company's point of view, and should be preceded by due diligence, which includes an analysis of supply and demand, an understanding of the drivers impacting the business and industry, and an examination of the financial implications. The *holding* or *retention period* is the time the space is held by the organization. During this period, facilities management and workplace management strategies are emphasized more than portfolio management, except for the important component of evaluation as the corporate real estate team will most likely be charged with assessing when the space is nearing the end of its utility. At that point, *disposition* represents the removal of the space from the portfolio through the ending of a leasehold or the sale of owned property. This will likely involve the execution of an exit strategy that is already in place for such eventualities.

This chapter is divided into three parts. The first addresses the need to understand factors impacting the acquisition of space, while the second considers the importance of analysis. The third section explores the value of implementation and evaluation to the management of the property life cycle.

Drivers

The acquisition, retention, and disposition of space is driven by a number of external business and economic factors. Before analyzing property-based factors, these industry and business-related drivers must be examined and weighed so that real estate priorities can be aligned with the underlying goals of the corporation.

As with many corporate real estate procedures, the process is often initiated with an expressed need. Either the overall organization or a specific business unit will request a new facility, whether that is office space, a manufacturing plant, a distribution warehouse, or retail location. Corporate real estate professionals then begin to consider how well this request aligns with the stated goals of the company and what type of flexibility the company may require in the future regarding these new assets. For example, a business unit leader may ask the real estate team to explore acquiring a new plant in Vermont, without knowing that the company has decided the regulatory environment is more favorable in South Carolina or that a merger is being discussed with a rival that holds significant assets in New England. Either of those scenarios would take the business unit's request out of alignment with corporate priorities.

While these drivers are under consideration, corporate real estate professionals must also understand the urgency of a request. A short-term, seasonal addition to the portfolio may be of little value if that season is over by the time all angles have been considered. Other external factors that may drive real estate decisions include:

- The addition or elimination of products or services

- The development or implementation of new technologies in the company or industry

- Market forces that impact the merits of leasing versus buying space

- The mitigation of—or appetite for—risk

- The state of financial markets and the financial arrangements needed for any acquisition

- Government or private incentives

- Demand for more sustainable or energy-efficient buildings

This list, which is not intended to be comprehensive, illustrates the variety of external factors that may influence what is acquired and how. Other considerations are more internal, including understanding:

- What business wants the space

- What the business intends to do with the space

- How long the space will be needed

- Whether the company treats real estate as an asset or a cost

• Where the space should be located

These considerations will be addressed in the following section.

Analysis (Costing)

Once external drivers have been identified and assessed, corporate goals must be understood so that corporate real estate decisions can be aligned with them. While it may seem as though all businesses have the same goals—to minimize costs while increasing income—this may be not be as straightforward as it first appears. A company may be in the midst of a strategic shift to more sustainable facilities, which may outweigh cost considerations. Another business may be making a long-term bet on a product line or region and thus have no interest in structuring the holding period to be as flexible as possible. For these reasons, the corporate real estate team must be closely aligned with the executive leadership team, with regular access and communication.

When these issues have been considered, a more intentional analysis, which includes an understanding of internal demand drivers as well as the available supply of space, can be successfully undertaken. This analysis

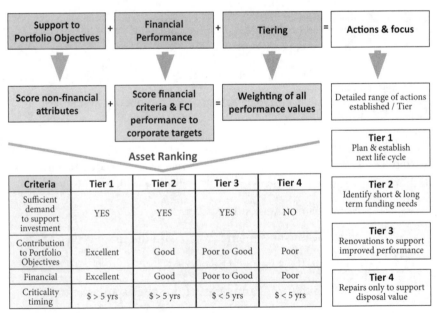

Figure 4.1 Assessing Life Cycle of Assets

enables professionals to watch for gaps, which may create the need for custom-built space and therefore lengthen the time it takes to get a new space up and running. Attention should also be paid to like-kind units or sub-portfolios, as one business unit may benefit from an acquisition being considered for another unit. The life cycle of assets within a corporate portfolio can be further grouped into tiers as shown in Figure 4.1 to reflect the assets' position with respect to financial and nonfinancial performance when compared to other assets in the portfolio.

Demand Forecasting

Demand forecasting includes a tally of existing space demand, measured in square feet / meters for manufacturing or distribution and number of users for office space, although different tasks may require different space allocations or projections per user. This tally is followed by a forecast of how the demand for space is likely to change—whether future use will be similar to existing needs, greater, or smaller. This assessment of expected changes, with input from the affected business units, can be translated into space demand—both the amount and type of space needed. Forecasts should take into account different possible scenarios, such as high-growth and low-growth outcomes, giving senior leadership different options to consider.

An analysis of supply should consider:

- The size of each type of space needed
- Space for lease versus sale
- Location of space
- Overall market conditions
- Type of space required (LEED, etc.)
- Efficiency of the space

This issue of efficiency can include sustainability concerns, functional obsolescence in older buildings, and the availability and reliability of utilities, as well as the suitability of the area's connectivity for its intended use. A gap analysis at the conclusion of this exercise should uncover holes in supply that might need to be filled with new construction or a reconsideration of locational needs.

Costing

Also, the total cost of the investment must be taken into account at this phase of the process. This assessment, sometimes called "costing," considers every cost-related aspect of adding or changing space within the portfolio from the cost of acquisition (leasing, buying, or building) to the operation of the facility and the efficiency of its systems, to utility costs and maintenance, and even move costs. The measurement of all costs related to the new space is needed in order to accurately measure it against other spaces, or existing options within the portfolio. This measurement should also include an educated guess as to the duration of the need, so that costs can hold up to the expected holding period.

Implementation and Evaluation

Completing the necessary analysis leads to implementation, or the acquisition of space. This phase brings to bear finance, site selection, transaction management, design, and build-out, and both quantitative and qualitative factors can influence the decision of which available space to acquire. As noted previously, duration matching can be another key factor, as long-term holds typically bring lower costs, leading professionals to prefer those if flexibility is not required.

During the holding period, a number of factors can help maximize the value of the asset and its return on investment at disposition. Efficient lease administration and facilities management will keep costs down and the space or building operating smoothly. These complicated processes can be mitigated by technology, in the form of appropriate software, and capable professionals specializing in these areas. Renewals may also need to be considered to keep the space in the fold beyond the initial leasehold period.

The life cycle of properties in the portfolio is always in flux and requires regular reconsideration and reevaluation. Properties must be evaluated on their ability to continue providing value to the enterprise both in the short and long term. This evaluation should consider market forces, such as whether market rent is above or below what is being paid for the space; the continuing usefulness of the space itself, which may include the question of whether a business unit still needs it; the cost of disposition and whether another business unit may benefit from the space; the financial needs of the organization; and any environmental considerations. As noted, this evaluation should be ongoing or repeated at regular intervals to ensure that surplus space does not linger on the books too long and that unnecessary costs (environmental, increased financing costs, etc.) can be avoided.

When the asset reaches the end of its economic usefulness to the enterprise, disposition comes into play, including environmental costs if required. Disposition may be called for because the space is underutilized or no longer needed, the operations for which it was intended have been discontinued, or it is no longer financially feasible to hold it. The corporate real estate professional should identify options and alternatives and prepare a plan for the disposal of properties that no longer provide value so the plan can be implemented quickly at that time. This can be accomplished by a variety of means, most often through the ending of a leasehold agreement or the sale of owned property. Other options include subleasing surplus space to minimize expenses, the auction or gifting of owned property, and pursuing a like-kind exchange with another party. The priority here is to gain the most value possible from the disposition or—if the space's economic utility is at an end for any company—to dispose of it at minimal cost to the organization.

Disposition represents the end of a property's life cycle, but the portfolio is likely to be in all phases of the life cycle at any given time. This makes it imperative that analysis, implementation, and evaluation be conducted regularly and repeated often enough to uncover unnecessary risks and expenses. Finance will always be a consideration in this process, and it is as much about risk as it is about costs. Occupancy cost is both a capital liability and an operational expense item, so there are many implications to consider. Any proposals for acquisitions or dispositions must address the chief financial officer's criteria. Managed properly, the property life cycle will keep corporate real estate professionals busy but also allow them to find cost savings on a consistent basis, adding value to the organization.

Conclusion

Seeing the portfolio through the lens of the property life cycle offers professionals a way to approach and manage change. In a portfolio of any size, change is an inevitable and constant factor in corporate real estate, as it is in other areas of the business such as technology or the workforce.

Businesses can be reactive, as many have been in the past, but leaders across most industries have discovered the value in planning ahead, forecasting demand, and responding to that need before it arises.

The property life cycle provides a data-driven rationale for the acquisition and disposition of space, as well as some techniques for measuring the utility of space during the holding period. For decades, real estate was seen largely as a necessary cost, and companies simply acquired and disposed of facilities based on a business unit's need, with little strategy behind the process. Today, corporate real estate is more widely accepted as a discipline that can manage some of the company's largest costs because the value of real estate assets can be increased by effective management of real estate as a resource.

As corporate real estate continues to unlock value in real estate and becomes more established in organizations, the real estate implications of business decisions are increasingly likely to be taken into account earlier in the process. Management of the entire property life cycle across the portfolio treats real estate as the valuable component it is, and alignment of those resources with the overall business strategy produces better products and services and strengthens the organization's bottom line.

Chapter 5

Real Estate Transactions and Leasing

Summary

One of the core functions of the corporate real estate team is managing real estate transactions, namely the purchase or lease of new property and disposing of property through a sale or lease termination. A single transaction will involve many different elements in terms of conducting due diligence, negotiating terms, arranging financing, obtaining the necessary internal approvals, and finalizing contracts. This chapter introduces the alternatives for structuring real estate transactions, such as capital leases, operating leases, purchases, and sale-leaseback arrangements.

Section one reviews some basic principles of corporate accounting and finance, particularly addressing the three basic financial statements: the income statement, balance sheet, and cash flow statement. Section two explores some of the fundamentals of real estate purchases and sales, as well as the pros and cons of buying versus leasing property. Section three addresses lease acquisition, lease administration, and lease strategy, while section four provides a brief summary of pending changes to lease accounting standards.

Fundamentals of Finance

Every organization, whether it is a public or private company, non-profit, or even a government agency, has a responsibility to its stakeholders. For-profit companies in particular are charged with the important task of delivering returns on shareholder investments. The long-term goal is to maximize stockholder wealth, while the short-term goal is to maximize profits. Publicly traded companies face the added challenge of balancing long- and short-term goals to meet analyst expectations. This section reviews some basic principles of corporate accounting and finance—the income statement, balance sheet, and cash flow statement—and discusses how real estate can impact those financial reporting tools. The affordability ratios often used to analyze real estate costs will also be explored.

The income statement, balance sheet, and cash flow statement form the heart of an annual report. These must conform to the standards of different regulatory boards such as the Financial Accounting Standards Board (FASB), Generally Accepted Accounting Principles (GAAP), International Accounting Standards Board (IASB), and International Financial Reporting Standards (IFRS). Publicly traded companies must follow reporting requirements of agencies related to their stock listings, such as the European Securities and Markets Authority or the Securities and Exchange Commission in the U.S.

Income Statement

The income statement reports the results of the corporation's activities over a period of time, such as quarterly or annually, in terms of revenues and expenses. It consists of three sections—revenue, expenses, and profits—or net income and earnings. Revenues are the inflow of new cash and receivables. Expenses are the outflow or costs associated with the revenue. Subtracting total expenses from total revenues results in a statement of profit or loss for the period, and these net profit or loss changes are carried to the statement of cash flows. Line items on an income statement that pertain specifically to real estate include rent or other occupancy expenses, depreciation of a property, and the operating interest expense for any related financing.

Balance Sheet

The balance sheet shows the financial status of the company at a specific point in time, listing the company's quantifiable resources and the claims against those resources by creditors and owners in terms of three sections—assets, liabilities, and equity. Owned property would be listed in the asset category, and any obligations against or financing related to the property would be recorded as liabilities.

The Cash Flow Statement

The cash flow statement describes all the changes that have occurred during the fiscal period in terms of cash. It shows where cash came from (sources) and where it went (uses) and includes three sections—operating activities, investing activities, and financing activities. The function of the cash flow statement is to reconcile the change in cash between the beginning of the accounting period and the end of the period.

Affordability Ratios

One of the goals of financial management is tracking the costs of the real estate the corporation uses for its business activities and keeping those costs in a desirable proportion to the corporation's revenue, expenses, assets, and liabilities. Affordability ratios are often used to help determine how much of the corporation's resources should be spent on its properties. The following affordability ratios can be used to compare the company's real estate costs with industry benchmarks, previous periods in the company's history, and competitor companies.

Occupancy expense as a percent of revenue. This measure shows how much revenue is consumed by occupancy costs: occupancy cost ÷ revenue.

Occupancy expense per person. Comparing occupancy costs with the number of employees is another way of measuring how efficiently the company uses its resources: occupancy cost ÷ full-time employees or full-time equivalents (FTEs).

Occupancy expense per square foot. This measure shows the cost per square foot /meter of the corporation's real estate holdings: occupancy cost ÷ square feet /square meters.

Revenue per square foot. Revenue per square foot /meter data is especially important in retail operations: revenue ÷ square feet /meters.

Real Estate Purchases and Sales

Purchasing, selling, and maintaining real estate can carry a hefty financial impact for a company. Even a single real estate transaction, such as the purchase or sale of a facility, can add up to millions and even tens of millions of dollars in profits—or losses. As discussed in the previous section, those financial decisions ripple through a company's income statement, balance sheet, and cash flow statement. This section provides a brief overview of some definitions and financial implications of a property purchase or sale. It will also look at alternative structures, such as the capital lease and sale-leaseback financing.

Property Purchase

A property purchase is a transaction that transfers to the buyer all ownership rights as well as legal title to a property. Along with the benefits of ownership, such as certain tax advantages and the potential accumulation of equity through appreciation, the buyer assumes all the risks and responsibilities of ownership. It is important to note that the laws related to transfer of title, as well as the responsibilities and rights of property owners, can vary widely from country to country.

The corporate real estate profession has long debated whether it is better to own or lease property. To provide the best answer to that question, a real estate professional needs a prudent estimate of how long the property is likely to be occupied along with a keen understanding of an organization's goals, strategy, situation, and location. The real estate team can help bring value to their organization by delivering a thorough analysis of the pros and cons of owning versus leasing that takes into consideration the pure real estate aspects as well as the organization's broader decision drivers and operational realities.

A property purchase generally involves a cash outlay and a mortgage loan. The owner-occupant assumes responsibility for all property operating costs, including taxes, insurance, repairs, maintenance, utilities, management, and interior finish.

The benefits of owning can include:

- Full control over use and tenure;
- No rent payments and protection from rent volatility;
- The prestige of ownership, which is important to some organizations;
- Potential asset appreciation, which could include benefits such as advantageous developments rights and /

or the increase in such development rights over time (e.g., permitted building density on the land is higher than what is built or may increase over time);

- Equity build-up from paying off portions of the loan; and

- A return of portions of the investment upon disposition.

The negative implications of owning can include:

- Potentially higher occupancy costs;

- Increased risk of liability;

- Illiquidity of capital tied up in real estate assets;

- Liability for capital costs, in particular as the asset grows older;

- Risk of having vacant space and not being able to rent it; and

- Risk that capital invested in the business itself may produce a higher rate of return than capital invested in a property.

Property Sale

In a sale, the seller conveys all rights and interests of ownership, along with title, to the buyer in exchange for a purchase price. The sale removes a fixed asset, the real estate, from the seller's balance sheet and may add to the seller's cash assets. Some of the common reasons to sell or dispose of an owned asset are to free up capital, relocate or consolidate operations, dissolve a losing business, cut expenses, or realize a capital gain. A property sale can be strategically advantageous if a company wants money to invest elsewhere. However, a sale also can have tax implications if there is a capital gain on the property.

Sale-leaseback

In a sale-leaseback transaction, the owner-operator sells a property or portfolio of properties and simultaneously enters into a lease with the buyer for the continued use of the property. The new lease is typically triple net, meaning the tenant pays for maintenance, taxes, and insurance as if it still owned the property.

The traditional motivations for undertaking a sale/leaseback are to free up capital "trapped" in the property, implement a disposition strategy, and reduce the degree of commitment and liability inherent in ownership. A sale-leaseback is an alternative financing source that allows an operator to get 100% of the value out of the real estate. Sale-leasebacks also can be used as a way to maximize asset sale price, in particular when market conditions are good and when demand is strong from investors seeking income-yielding property. In addition, sale-leasebacks can be a useful way to dispose of a property that will soon be redundant (e.g., one that will not be required in two to three years).

Lease Acquisitions

Leasing strategy and lease administration often fall under the broader category of "portfolio optimization" as companies seek to "right-size" real estate. Leasing is a form of financing to pay for only the amount of real estate needed for a specific period of time.

Companies that desire shorter occupancy terms or to retain cash and financing leverage tend to prefer to lease versus own their real estate. Shorter lease terms, such as one-, two-, or three-year terms, can help a company adapt to changing operations. Leases also can be negotiated to enhance flexibility with more frequent or earlier termination dates, expansion and exit clauses, and renewal options. Flexibility rights, such as options for expansion, can be particularly important in markets with high ongoing demand. Coordinating the end dates of leases, subleases, and exit clauses in adjacent spaces also allows organizations to shift or disband operations.[1]

As with real estate acquisitions, the laws governing lease transactions vary from country to country. In Brazil, for example, lease documents are relatively short, approximately 10 pages, because lease laws are defined by Brazilian federal laws. In comparison, lease documents in the U.S. can exceed 100 pages in some cases because lease provisions, clauses, and rights are often described in detail. So, it is important to have local knowledge regarding lease practices and laws in a particular location.

Operating Lease

An operating lease transfers certain rights to occupy and use a property to a tenant while leaving the major risks and benefits of ownership with the landlord / owner. In acquiring an operating lease, a tenant incurs a financial obligation to pay rent over the lease term, and the lease may require other periodic payments for occupancy-related items such as utilities, common area expenses, taxes, insurance, and maintenance.

An operating lease does not require the capital outlay of a purchase transaction, leaving the company relatively more liquid and flexible. There can be capital outlays required for tenant improvements made to leased space, which are typically capitalized and depreciated over the term of the lease. A second benefit of an operating lease is that the company can expense, or deduct, the full rent payment for tax purposes.

Capital Lease

A capital lease, also referred to as a finance lease, is a long-term leasing agreement that is recorded on financial statements as if it were a purchase. This hybrid structure has characteristics of both a purchase and a lease. A capital lease is like any lease in that a lessee makes rent payments to a lessor, who continues to own the property. The transaction is like a purchase in that the lease conveys so much of the useful life and / or value of the property to the lessee over time that the lessee, rather than the lessor, is effectively receiving the benefits of ownership. In this arrangement, the lease payments are akin to loan payments in a long-term financing arrangement, or to installment payments in an installment sale.

Lease Accountancy Standards

Corporations are facing a significant change to traditional lease accounting practices. The existing accounting models for leases require lessees to classify their leases as either capital leases or operating leases. Traditionally, capital leases have received on-balance sheet treatment, while operating leases have received off-balance sheet treatment. Meaning, tenants with operating leases do not have to report those financial obligations as liabilities on their balance sheets. The model has been criticized by some for its lack of transparency for analysts and investors; however, the operating lease obligations have always been disclosed in the notes to the published financial statements.

For a number of years, the Financial Accounting Standards Board and the International Accounting Standards Board have been working on a joint proposal to create new accounting rules for lease transactions. The intent is to create greater transparency in how companies record leases on their balance sheets. The proposed lease accounting changes will remove the distinction between finance leases and operating leases. Operating leases would be recognized both on the asset side as a right of use asset and the present value of payments during the lease term will be recognized as a liability.[2] Ultimately, what that means for corporations is that lease liabilities will appear more prominently in corporate financial statements.

For U.S. public companies alone, those changes have the potential to impact an estimated $1.3 trillion in corporate real estate obligations and liabilities not represented on the balance sheet, according to the U.S. Securities and Exchange Commission and based on 2009 data. Firms with a large real estate portfolio of leased real estate will see the biggest impact. In particular, banks, retailers, restaurants, and other service businesses with hundreds of locations are concerned about the added lease administrative and data management burden. At publication time, the new accounting rules were expected to go into effect within a few years but will require two comparison years prior to the effective date.

The accounting change can have real impacts on corporate real estate activities and on the systems used to manage real estate portfolios: financial transaction systems; real estate management systems; enterprise asset management systems; financial planning, budgeting, and forecasting systems; and tax planning and compliance systems. Companies also may be less willing to carry unproductive or underutilized real estate assets when they consider the impact those leases will have on the balance sheet. According to a 2014 survey of finance executives conducted jointly by CFO Research and IBM, two-thirds of finance executives believe the proposed changes to lease accounting standards will make it more important to optimize real estate portfolios, such as consolidating or disposing of underutilized assets.[3]

Many firms have already implemented new lease tracking systems to more efficiently manage lease information. In addition, there is some speculation that the changing regulatory issues could spark a broader "catalyst for change" in the real estate decision-making process.[2] Those changes could prompt some firms to develop new strategies to measure the impact of the new lease accounting standards on decisions related to owning versus leasing, lease duration, real estate utilization, company outsourcing, and supply-chain management, among other factors.

Conclusion

Real estate professionals need to be very aware of the financial implications of various transactions. Buying, selling, or leasing property can represent both a significant financial opportunity and sizable financial risk for an organization. Overall, this chapter provides a reference guide to basic financial terms and different options for structuring transactions.

References

1. Apgar, M. (2009, Nov. 30). What every leader should know about real estate. The Economist Intelligence Unit in partnership with Harvard Business School Publishing. *Harvard Business Review.* Retrieved from https://hbr.org/2009/11/what-every-leader-should-know-about-real-estate.

2. Schelle, T., Baltussen, S., Van Leersum, L., & Appel-Meulenbroek, R. (2013, July/August). Lease accounting as a catalyst to change corporate real estate decision making. *The LEADER.* Retrieved from https://resources.corenetglobal.org/knowledgecenteronline/SearchByTopicAndResource.aspx?ID=4372

3. CFO Research. (2014). *Working smart: Value management for corporate real estate.* A report prepared by CFO Research in collaboration with IBM. Retrieved from http://www.google.com/url?sa=t&rct=j&q=&esrc=s&source=web&cd=1&ved=0CC4QFjAAahUKEwjPrLHzoZLGAhULJqwKHRWdAHU&url=http%3A%2F%2Fwww.gocfi.com%2Fwp-content%2Fuploads%2F2015%2F06%2FWorking-Smart-Value-Mgmt-for-Corp-Real-Estate.pdf&ei=0hB_Vc_7D4vMsAWVuoKoBw&usg=AFQjCNHriYVOIgBxZnRVpoGfoBaCgPXlLw&cad=rja

Chapter 6

Finance

Summary

From a finance perspective, real estate can be both an asset and a liability. It also can represent a significant cost center for many organizations. In order to make real estate decisions or recommendations to company leaders, real estate executives need to fully understand the financial risks. What is the potential value and cost both today and in the future? Such financial analysis can relate to the acquisition and disposition of property, leasing or renewal decisions, new construction and capital expenditure projects, and the ongoing operation of real estate.

This chapter, which features five sections, provides an introduction to some of the key finance concepts used in corporate real estate portfolio management and strategy. Section one provides a summary of how real estate performs as a financial instrument. Section two addresses how finance links to portfolio strategy and how a broader financial understanding can help corporate real estate professionals be more effective. A brief overview on how corporate real estate decisions impact company profitability and competitive advantage is provided in section three, while section four introduces key terms and formulas frequently used in financial analysis of real estate. Section five features a case study that illustrates the financial implications of two different lease scenarios.

What Is Real Estate Finance?

Managing costs has long been a priority for corporate real estate professionals. Real estate can be leased or held as an investment or an owner-occupied asset; each option commits the beneficiary to a financial liability and a corresponding asset or benefit. Over the past decade, corporations have increasingly seen real estate as a financial instrument to either drive cost-savings opportunities or even generate added revenues.

Real estate can be both a financial asset and liability. As an asset, it enables work to take place, attracts the right type of employee talent, and provides proximity to customers, suppliers, and competitors. On the other hand, as a liability, it locks in a medium- to long-term cost commitment, adds cost to overhead, and might tie up capital that could otherwise be invested into the core business activity.

Real estate as a place of work is typically a company's second- or third-largest cost on an income statement and balance sheet. According to a 2014 research study conducted by CFO Research and IBM, more than half (55%) of finance executives surveyed place real estate among the four largest components of corporate operating costs.[1] As a result, corporate real estate professionals need to ensure that they have a sound understanding of how the costs and value associated with real estate impact a company's profitability and resource allocation. To understand this better, we must first look to the principles of general financial management within an organization.

Financial management is based on understanding how much a company can spend, assuming how much it is earning and how much it costs to run the business. In order for finance professionals to assess this dynamic, they must undertake financial planning and analysis to determine the priorities for investing the company's cash and using the company's working capital. The goal is to deliver an economic benefit while limiting the amount of money committed on a year-over-year basis to leasing or financing costs of occupied real estate. The management of financial resources, therefore, involves allocating a company's capital on the basis of a return and managing overheads as part of cash flow and working capital management.

From an investment perspective, a company will only invest in an asset or building when it can prove it cannot get a better return from some other opportunity, such as research and development, product or service line growth, or entrance into a new market. So, as an investment, real estate must demonstrate through the acquisition price and ongoing running costs that it can produce a return, typically through sub-let income or through capital appreciation (an increase in the worth of the property on the open market).

From an occupier perspective, corporate real estate executives view real estate costs as a factor of utility or production. To that point, consideration needs to be given to the company's time and price commitment relative to how much it can afford to pay considering its income.

In order to determine the best option when confronted with different projects, corporate real estate professionals use financial formulas and analysis to understand the financial impact of those projects on the organization. These include formulas to:

- Project cash flow over a period of time
- Use the discount rate to reflect risk
- Calculate net present value (NPV)
- Calculate the internal rate of return (IRR)
- Calculate the economic value added (EVA)
- Calculate payback period (if appropriate)

These terms will be covered in more detail later in the chapter.

Why Is Finance Important to Corporate Real Estate Professionals?

As a corporate real estate professional, you will be concerned either with how real estate acts as a financial instrument for investment or how real estate provides corporate occupiers with an effective place to do business. This chapter focuses primarily on corporate real estate as a corporate occupier. Corporate real estate professionals are often responsible for finding property solutions for business needs and supporting local business units by understanding how choices in location, building type, floor plate, and size of building can support a company's strategic objectives, which may include growing in a particular geography, attracting and retaining the right type of talent, or proximity to its customers. Real estate selection should also be based on what is financially prudent for a particular business.

Cost control can be managed in a number of ways when procuring real estate. For example, a corporate real estate professional can:

- Negotiate the best deal possible and reduce the rate per square foot / meter payable on a building's rent.

- Advise on a smaller floor plate to accommodate the same number of staff using innovative technical and workplace design solutions to achieve increased space utilization and efficiency.

- Reduce service provisions or renegotiate contracts with workplace and facility suppliers to bring down the cost of management services and / or service charges.

Overall, it is important for corporate real estate professionals to fully understand all associated costs to create a total occupancy cost perspective and determine the cash flow implications in building a compelling business case for a particular scenario, such as the lease or acquisition of a property.

Why Is Finance Important to an Organization?

As corporate real estate professionals become more sophisticated in understanding how real estate impacts an organization's overall financial performance and strategy, they also are becoming increasingly interested in learning how real estate can support the financial objectives of an organization. A number of key concepts and priorities pertain to financial analysis and strategy related to managing costs, as well as to the financial implications of structuring properties for sale or lease.

As previously mentioned, real estate is one of the largest factors relating to an organization's profits and losses, and, as a result, finance directors are constantly looking for ways to reduce the costs associated with real estate. As mentioned in the last section, this can be delivered through reducing floor plates, reducing the amount spent on facilities and service charges, managing energy costs, consolidating building space, and using workplace solutions to derive more cost-effective use of buildings. In addition, real estate costs sit within the fixed costs section of the profit and loss reports, which drives down net margin or core operating profit in large corporations. The smaller your overhead, the bigger your net margin and the better your profit. As a result, finance directors are eager to maximize revenue and minimize fixed costs.

Options for selling property can also produce different financial results for an organization. Owned assets can be sold either with vacant possession or with a retained lease (a sale-leaseback of the property) to generate capital profits for an organization. Such capital profits are referred to as "trade receivables" or "other trading income." Proceeds from a sale can be used for reinvestment into core business operations that generate a higher return than the capital return being delivered through a building-related investment.

In the sale-leaseback of a property, the tenant or seller can choose whether they will have the right for the asset to revert to them at the end of the lease or have a first right of refusal in the event of a property sale to a third party. Which option a seller chooses could alter the price significantly. For example, securing an option to buy the property back will reduce the value on the open market and therefore reduce the value of the cash flow to a third party, which means a lower initial sale price.

Consideration should also be given as to whether lease agreements to rent space are structured as a finance or an operating lease. A finance lease provision will sit on the balance sheet like a capital asset and be depreciated over a period of time, whereas an operating lease will only show in the annual profit and loss to which costs are attributable. [The distinction between operating leases and capital leases may be removed in the future with the adoption of International Financial Reporting Standards (e.g., from the International Accounting Standards Board, or IASB) and hence all future leases may all be functionally equivalent to debt, thereby driving interest expense up, eliminating rental payment expense, and impacting debt ratios and bank debt covenants.]

Key Real Estate Finance Terms, Concepts, and Formulas

This section provides a brief summary of key real estate finance concepts, terms, and formulas used by finance and real estate professionals alike. For further detailed information please refer to *Property Finance* by David Isaac.[2]

Evaluation of real estate decisions (e.g., lease versus purchase) involves complex and differing cash flows over a long period of time. Financial analysis allows the corporate real estate professional and finance professional to reduce that complexity so that decisions can be made when comparing alternative projects.

In analyzing the impact of real estate on a corporation's financial situation, it is necessary to consider what is known as the "time value of money." The basis of this concept is that an amount of money projected to be paid or received at some time in the future does not have the same value as that money does today. Few companies let their capital sit idle. Organizations tend to put that money to work in their own business or through different investment alternatives that generate a return. Another strong incentive for putting money to work is the simple fact that, if it does sit idle, its value will deteriorate due to inflationary pressure. Whether buying a gallon of milk or weighing construction costs, prices rise, and $1 USD today does not have the same buying power that it did a year ago.

The basic principles of time value of money are:

- **Present value:** A dollar tomorrow is worth less than a dollar today.

- **Future value:** A dollar today is worth more than a dollar tomorrow.

In both cases, compounding amplifies that effect, which means the more time that passes with no investment, the bigger the loss, and likewise, the more time that passes with a steady return on that investment, the bigger the gain.

For example, if you have one dollar available to use today, you can invest it somewhere, such as buying stocks or bonds, and earn a return on that dollar. If, for example, you loan that dollar to a friend and charge him 5% interest per year, then that dollar will be worth $1.28 USD after five years. That amount is the future value of one dollar compounded for five years at 5%. If you want to know the value of one dollar to be received or paid at a time five years in the future, you have to discount the future value (one dollar) to its present value in the same way. Using 5% as the discount rate, its present value is only $.78 USD. Put that concept into a real estate context and the basic principle is that:

• a dollar of rent paid today is more expensive than a dollar paid in the future, and a dollar paid in the future is less expensive than a dollar paid today.

Net Present Value and Internal Rate of Return Practices

The finance team often uses net present value calculations or analyses to compare and contrast the return on investment of two different scenarios. For example, what is the best financial option when choosing between a lease that will cost more in rent in the later years versus a lease that has more gradual rental rate increases throughout the term of a lease? In addition, net present value calculations do not necessarily mean that an organization's leadership will automatically choose the option with the most favorable net present value.

For example, an organization might use net present value in its financial analysis to compare the cost of leasing space in two different office buildings. Option A is located one block from a subway station and also includes amenities such as a fitness center and on-site food service. Option B is located four blocks from the same subway station and has no fitness center or on-site restaurants. All other building features are more or less equal. Because of its added features, Option A has a higher rent—$30 USD per square foot compared to $28 USD per square foot at Option B. In this case, the company may decide to choose the more expensive building with more convenience and amenities, but they also have a clear picture of how much those additional features will cost over the course of the lease.

Some alternatives to net present value include the payback period and the internal rate of return. The payback period is the length of time required to recoup initial investment. This method encourages quick return of capital, and it may not be advantageous if capital is invested profitably. It also ignores the size of the investment and the time value of money. For example, a real estate team may use internal rate of return to calculate the return or payback on investing capital in sustainable building features, such as a new low-flow water system or a more efficient heating system.

Internal rate of return is the discount rate that results in an investment having a net present value equal to zero. Similar to the payback period, internal rate of return also ignores the size of the investment and duration of investment. In addition, some cash flow streams have multiple internal rates of return—or none at all.

Discount Rate

One of the key variables in real estate finance is the discount rate. It is important to have an understanding of the discount rate in order to discuss calculations for net present value and internal rate of return later in this chapter. The discount rate is the "opportunity cost" of capital. The discount rate is the potential return that could have been earned if the capital were used for investment elsewhere, such as invested back into the core business or in alternative investments such as stocks or bonds.

The discount rate used by an individual company to evaluate financial decisions is usually set by the corporate finance team. Some firms use multiple discount rates to reflect differing risk profiles of various cash flow components in property decisions. For example, contractually, certain cash flows, such as lease payments or tax savings from depreciation, could be discounted at the firm's operating discount rate. Residual interests, such as terminal value or sublease rents, could be discounted at a rate reflecting speculative real estate market risk.

Net Present Value (NPV)

The net present value determines the profitability or cost of an investment by looking at all cash flows, both inflows and outflows. The result is always in today's dollars.

The net present value rules. Corporate real estate managers normally would accept all projects that are worth more than they cost. In general, a positive net present value is favorable, and the higher the positive net present value, the better. However, it is important to note that real estate does not always generate a positive net present value. For example, a lease decision may force a corporate real estate professional to select the "least negative" net present value.

There are four steps in the net present value decision model process:

- Forecast the future net cash flow
- Determine the discount rate (usually provided by the finance team)
- Calculate the present value of the future net cash flows
- Net present value = present value minus the initial investment

Internal Rate of Return (IRR)

If you know the present or future value of an investment, such as an owned property, plus the timing and amount of any cash inflows and outflows generated by the property, you can use a calculator to determine the internal rate of return (IRR) of the property, which is the discount rate at which all the cash outflows equal the cash inflows, or when net present values are assumed to equal zero. The IRR is also the expected rate of return of the project or investment. The project or investment alternative with the higher IRR is generally the preferred, from a financial perspective

The internal rate of return rules. The internal rate of return is not the same as cost of capital. When using internal rate of return rules, choose the project when internal rate of return is greater than or equal to the cost of capital. Here are the steps in the decision process:

- Internal rate of return = discount rate at which the net present value equals 0

- When internal rate of return is greater than the cost of capital, the net present value is greater than 0.

- When internal rate of return is less than the cost of capital, net present value is less than 0.

Case Study Examples

Life cycle costing (LCC), is a technique to establish the total cost of ownership. The results of an LCC analysis can be used to assist a company in the decision-making process where there is a choice of options. The accuracy of LCC analysis diminishes as it projects further into the future, so it is most valuable as a comparative tool when long-term assumptions apply to all the options and consequently have the same impact. For example, imagine that the capital expenditure (CAPEX) for an energy conservation project is $2 million USD, resulting in an annual cost saving of approximately $200,000 USD a year for the next 20 years. In addition, assume a discount rate of 10%.

Given these figures, is the project a good investment? Superficially, it looks to be a good proposition; that is, an initial investment of $2 million USD results in an eventual cost saving of $4 million USD. However, by calculating the present value (PV) of the recurring cost savings against the initial capital expenditure, the cost saving benefit is calculated to be $1,702,713 USD or approximately $300,000 USD less than the original capital investment. It is therefore unlikely that this project would be approved.

However, would the same decision apply if the discount rate were 6%? The revised results indicate an accumulated cost saving of $2,293,984 USD, now signifying a favorable investment. Under these conditions, the project is likely to be approved, although the final decision would probably reflect the company's confidence (or lack of it) in either discount rate.

As a second example, assume a manager is tasked to investigate complaints concerning noisy, expensive to operate, and unreliable air-conditioning. The investigations indicate that the equipment is beyond economic repair and needs replacing, and three potential alternatives have been selected: a variable-air-volume (VAV) system; a dual conduit system; and a dual duct VAV system (see Table 6.1). Each system has technical advantages. Each also has LCC implications.

If we assume a 25-year time period and a discount rate of 3.5%, the net present value (NPV) for each system is equivalent to summing the

	VAV System	Dual Conduit System	Dual Duct VAV System
Life cycle	15 years	15 years	20 years
Implementation costs	$792,000 USD	$891,000 USD	$1,108,500 USD
Annual maintenance cost	$72,000 USD	$84,000 USD	$96,000 USD
Annual energy costs	$432,000 USD	$480,000 USD	$528,000 USD
Annual energy savings due to adaptive control	$48,000 USD	$48,000 USD	$36,000 USD
Annual energy savings due to variable speed drive control	$96,000 USD	$72,000 USD	$48,000 USD
Salvage @ 25 years	$79,200 USD	$89,100 USD	$110,850 USD

Table 6.1. Three Alternative Air-Conditioning Systems

present value for the initial and replacement equipment costs, plus the present value of all recurring costs (maintenance and energy) and deducting the present value of the energy savings as well as the present value of the salvage. Thus, for the VAV system, NPV = ($7,164,569); for the dual control system, NPV = ($8,702,920); and for the dual duct VAV system, NPV = ($10,518,706). Given these NPV cost calculations, the recommendation would be to select the variable air volume system.

However, would the same decision be made assuming energy costs escalate by 2% over inflation? Recalculating the figures, the NPV for the VAV system = ($8,406,338); for dual control system, NPV = ($10,255,130); and for dual duct VAV system, NPV = ($12,433,099) respectively. Hence, irrespective of energy escalation, the VAV system is the preferred system in terms of its LCC assessment. (Significantly, energy costs account for almost two-thirds of the total NPV in all three cases, whereas the salvage value represents a mere 0.5% NPV.)

References

1. CFO Research. (2014). *Working smart: Value management for corporate real estate*. A report prepared by CFO Research in collaboration with IBM. Retrieved from http://www.google.com/url?sa=t&rct=j&q=&esrc=s&source=web&cd=1&ved=0CC4Q FjAAahUKEwjPrLHzoZLGAhULJqwKHRWdAHU&url=http%3A%2F%2Fwww. gocfi.com%2Fwp-content%2Fuploads%2F2015%2F06%2FWorking-Smart-Value-Mgmt-for-Corp-Real-Estate.pdf&ei=0hB_Vc_7D4vMsAWVuoKoBw&usg=AF QjCNHriYVOIgBxZnRVpoGfoBaCgPXlLw&cad=rja

2. Isaac, D. (2003). *Property Finance* (2nd ed.). Palgrave Macmillan.

Chapter 7

Organizational Models, Service Delivery,

and Outsourcing

Summary

A discussion about how corporate real estate organizations deliver services to the corporation and internal business clients starts with how the corporate real estate department "fits" within the overall corporate enterprise. What is the operating model? Is responsibility for corporate real estate centralized in a single department? Or is it decentralized, at least in part, with some functions delivered through various business units or other parts of the corporation? And does corporate real estate have a "mandate"? In other words, must the business utilize the services of the corporate real estate organization?

Also important is how the corporate real estate department is organized. Most corporate real estate groups are organized either by function (e.g., facility management, portfolio management, etc.), by geography (e.g., North America, Asia-Pacific, Europe, Middle East and Africa, etc.) or a hybrid – some combination of function and geography.

In addition, an important strategic consideration for corporate real estate is to determine which functions should be handled directly by the internal corporate real estate team, and which functions are best delivered by external service provider companies. There is no single best answer, or one-size-fits-all solution.

At one time, before the corporate real estate outsourcing marketplace was established and began to grow (i.e., in the early- to mid-1990s), many corporations had large corporate real estate departments. The majority of real estate services work was done in-house.

As the scale and capabilities of the service provider market have grown over the past 20 years, and as companies have seen the benefits of working with external partners, the trend has been toward increasingly smaller, leaner internal corporate real estate departments that directly provide portfolio strategy, customer relationship management and vendor management, with tactical delivery (and, increasingly, even some more strategic functions) provided by external real estate service provider partners. Yet even today, some major multinational corporations maintain relatively large real estate organizations and utilize outsourcing only on a limited basis.

For the majority of large, global corporations, working in partnership with real estate service providers is an important part of their service-delivery strategy. As a result, following a discussion of corporate real estate operating models, much of this chapter is devoted to a discussion of corporate real estate outsourcing.

The Internal Corporate Real Estate Organization

The most common operating models for corporate real estate are the Direct or Center-Led Model, the Indirect or Advisory Model, and the Influence Model.[1]

1. **Direct or Center-Led Model** – In this model, all corporate real estate employees within a company report up through a single, global lead. The model is described as "fully integrated," as there is a single real estate function for the entire company. Regardless of geography or functional area, corporate real estate is structured as a centralized organization and drives strategy, policy, process, technology, and performance management in a standardized manner globally. In addition, customer relationship management and supplier/vendor management is centrally coordinated.

2. **Indirect or Advisory Model** – With the indirect or advisory model, part of the corporate real estate function

is centralized and reports directly into a global head. Additional corporate real estate employees are aligned by the business unit and/ or by geography and report into local business operations. The functional or geographically aligned staffs typically have a dotted-line relationship to the worldwide head for corporate real estate, hence the "indirect" nomenclature. Corporate real estate drives strategy, policy, process, technology, and performance management from a centralized organization, but adoption of these standards by the field is voluntary.

3. **Influence Model** – This model provides for a small "center of excellence" that provides corporate real estate advisory services to the corporation's various business units. In this model, the corporate real estate group does not control the resources that execute the work, as these resources are aligned to local business unit operations. The business units are usually not required to leverage the knowledge or expertise of the corporate real estate group, though this is certainly encouraged. Of these three models, the "influence" model presents the most challenges in terms of enforcing global standards for strategy, policy, process, technology, and performance management.

The decision to adopt a particular type of operating model and organizational structure is dependent on several contributing factors. These include: (1) the maturity of the corporate real estate organization, (2) the complexity of the overall enterprise, (3) the industry context (i.e., financial services versus high technology), (4) the scope of services, (5) the geographic distribution of operations, and (6) the chosen service delivery model (i.e., outsourced, out-tasked, in-house, or hybrid delivery).

As corporate real estate departments and their companies evolve and better appreciate the benefits of effective asset planning and management, they typically trend towards a direct or center-led model. Over time, the direct model supports easier transition to the highly leveraged, outsourced service delivery models that many companies are adopting.

As the use of external resources to support corporate real estate service delivery became more common, the corporate-provider relationships in many instances transitioned from vendor agreements, to preferred supplier agreements, to strategic alliance relationships, and finally to strategic partnerships.[1]

Outsourcing Corporate Real Estate Services

This section will discuss a number of important issues related to corporate real estate outsourcing, beginning with perhaps the most important question: Why would companies choose to outsource?

Why Companies Outsource

According to approximately 200 end users and service providers surveyed for a 2013 Deloitte/CoreNet Global report on outsourcing, the primary drivers for outsourcing are cost reduction, need to focus on more strategic activities, a desire for increased flexibility, and a chance to gain leading practices.[2]

Cost reduction, focus. Not surprisingly, cost reduction ranks highest among primary drivers (as it historically does across most industries), followed closely by the need to focus on more strategic activities. Outsourcing provides two types of cost reduction. First, an organization's costs are reduced if it does not to have to maintain a large internal staff to deliver real estate facilities management services. Second, outsourced partners will have the ability to deliver services more efficiently and leverage buying power and procurement rigor across all areas of spending (e.g., rent, operating expenses, and facility costs).

Increased flexibility. When a company's employees are focused on their core competencies, the enterprise becomes more nimble and responsive. The outsourcing model also allows for scalability, allowing an outsourced partner to expand its operations without adding corresponding numbers in the contracting company.

Leading Practices. Finally, outsourcing allows companies to gain leading practices and expertise. When an organization's outsourcing partners are the top in their fields, the work they do for that end user will establish the benchmarks (best practices) for those tasks, which are increasingly in critical arenas of the company's operations. The service providers will also apply resources in the form of time and funding to develop more innovative technologies and tools to further enhance the service delivery.

Not surprisingly, a corporate end user that undertakes outsourcing has high expectations. According to the 2013 KPMG Global Real Estate & Facilities Management Outsourcing Pulse Survey, "A typical end-user organization's expectations are that outsourcing will improve their operational model, introduce leading practices, and drive continuous improvement."[3]

Why Companies Don't Outsource

While the trend points toward more outsourcing, there are reasons a company would choose not to do so. According to the nearly 200 end users and service providers who participated in the 2013 Deloitte/CoreNet Global report on outsourcing, among the top reasons not to outsource are organizational resistance, risk transfer, cost, lack of trust, and lack of flexibility.[2]

Organizational resistance. Organizations—especially private companies—tend to develop a certain level of institutional inertia as they grow, and high-level executives often view even less-than-ideal outcomes as preferable to the unknown. Frequently, this mindset is cultural and goes beyond the corporate real estate department. Whether a company has been successful in outsourcing other functions (e.g., procurement, HR) can influence its decision to outsource real estate functions.

Risk transfer. It makes sense that a company might be wary of outsourcing crucial functions to an outside party because it faces significant risks if things do not go well. This concern is more prevalent among companies affected by regulatory bodies and with high infrastructure costs (i.e., for asset classes such as industrial or research and development).

Cost. While any successful outsourcing agreement is no doubt delivering a positive bottom-line impact (after all, "cost savings" is traditionally the top reason *to* outsource), companies can view such an initiative as entailing a net cost increase—at least initially.

Lack of trust. An end user accustomed to—and comfortable with—entrusting its own people to execute most business operations could be hesitant to pass off control to outside parties.

Lack of flexibility. Some organizations are structured in such a way that it would make it difficult to easily transfer responsibility for certain tasks from in-house personnel to an external company.

No compelling reason. According to the 2013 KPMG survey, the most commonly noted reason not to outsource was "no compelling business case" (cited by 64% of end user respondents in the Americas). Following that rationale closely were the ideas that a company's activities "are too strategic in nature" and that "costs would be higher."[3]

What Is Outsourced Most and Least Often

Overall, the three areas most commonly outsourced to a third party are:

- Lease administration (e.g., lease abstracting, lease document administration, portfolio analysis, performance reporting);

- Transaction management (e.g., acquiring or disposing of leased or owned space); and

- Facilities management (physical management of facilities).

According to the 2013 KPMG survey, lease abstracting was the activity most commonly outsourced in the lease administration category (cited by 77% of respondents), followed by data entry and administration of lease documents and critical data reporting and tracking (both cited by 68% of respondents).[3] The outsourcing of lease abstracting ranked highest in the 2012 edition of the KPMG study, while critical data entry rose from No. 4 to No. 2 in the 2013 study.[3]

In the arena of facilities management, a subset area is workplace services (e.g., janitorial, cafeteria, and amenities services), and it is this part of real estate facilities management that companies most often choose to outsource. It was fully outsourced by 69% of end-user respondents in the

KPMG survey and partially outsourced by an additional 22%. Only 4% outsource no tasks in this area.[3]

Also frequently outsourced—and also under the facilities management umbrella—is facilities services (e.g., HVAC, electrical, mechanical, and building repair). A total of 91% of respondents report fully outsourcing this category, with only 4% responding, "not at all."[3]

In terms of least-outsourced functions, only 30% of end-user respondents in the KPMG survey have completely or partially outsourced portfolio strategy and planning of real estate facilities management.[3] This is an unsurprising finding as most companies historically have deemed these areas "core" responsibilities that are best delivered by experienced and senior executives—internal employees who have the deepest knowledge and understanding of the subject, along with established relationships with the organization's leadership.

Tendency to Outsource Varies by Industry Sector

According to service providers and third-party advisors who responded to the 2013 KPMG survey (and reflecting rankings identical to 2012), banking, financial services, and insurance were most likely to outsource real estate and facilities services (cited by 56% of respondents), followed by health care (34%), and pharma / biotech (29%).[3]

Particular industries' tendency to outsource is related to the nature of their real estate portfolios. For instance, banking, financial services, and insurance entities often have high-count, geographically dispersed, homogeneous, but rapidly changing facility needs that are often well served by one of the outsourcing models. On the other hand, other types of business tend to have high infrastructure requirements that are core to their business, and as such, are perhaps not ideally outsourced.

Outsourcing Models

While outsourcing in corporate real estate currently is *de rigueur* for most large entities, some firms take an in-between step of "out-tasking" a specific function within a department to another company instead of outsourcing of a department's entire function. If companies are ready to take the full outsourcing step, they achieve their outsourcing goals via several different models and structures.

- **Multiple service providers (best in class).** This model involves finding the ideal service provider for the task, which can result in multiple service providers for various tasks. This framework requires a moderate staffing level within the retained organization to coordinate—enough to stay connected to the business while overseeing the actions of the outsourcing partners to ensure performance.

- **Single service provider (bundled).** This single-source solution entails one service provider delivering multiple services. The term "bundled" can also mean aggregating several related tasks under one provider. For example facilities maintenance tasks like janitorial work, landscaping, and trash removal might be bundled with one provider, while corporate real estate services, such as planning, property administration, brokerage, project management, and activity coordination, might all be performed by another. The delineation would be based on function, as opposed to the company's business units.

- **Integrated.** A hybrid, and relatively new approach, known as the integrator model, is one in which a single, main service provider—the integrator—manages a host of other service providers.

Both the single-provider model and multiple-provider model have existed for years, and there are many examples of large corporate occupiers who use one approach or the other successfully. In a 2012 Cushman & Wakefield Client Perspective survey, 31% of responding occupiers reported that they use a single service provider, 39% use two or three service providers, and 30% use four or more service providers.[4]

Single-Provider Model Case Study

State Street Corporation (SSC), a global investment-services provider with nearly 30,000 employees in 29 countries, opted for a single-provider approach almost exclusively when it revamped its corporate real estate outsourcing beginning in 2005.

The challenge, according to a case study appearing in the article "Service Delivery and Outsourcing" in a 2012 issue of *The Leader*, "was to take an integrated facilities management (IFM) service-delivery model that was self-performed, with extensive out-tasking, and consolidate all of the services under one IFM service agreement."[5]

When each outsourced portion was originally put out to bid over a seven-year period, SSC awarded the management of larger chunks of its worldwide corporate real estate operations to a large, global provider. By 2011, SSC's global holdings topped 7.4 million square feet, and the company had turned over 65 percent of its integrated facilities management services to outside providers. A regional service provider was tapped to handle the EMEA region (Europe, Middle East and Africa)—roughly 14% of the portfolio—while a global service provider handled the rest.

As SSC handed over each additional piece of its portfolio, its employees renegotiated pricing under a consolidated contract with the global provider, resulting in lower costs and more consistent service delivery. In addition, a global technology platform was implemented that further improved standard business processes and management reporting.

Multiple-Provider Model

Advantages. For some companies, competitive pressures have made best-in-class outsourcing models with multiple service providers more attractive. As noted in the article "The Polygamy of CRE Outsourcing" in the March/April 2014 issue of *The Leader*:

> The once common practice of using a single-service provider for all of a company's corporate real estate needs is becoming increasingly less common. Corporates are valuing the expert relationships they have built in their various geographies and business lines, as opposed to a turnkey practice of using a single source. These relationships allow them to tap into best practices and a local knowledge base without being married to just one provider.[6]

This approach does require internal procurement and ongoing management of in-house staff to maintain the best-in-class model.

In that same *Leader* article, Cristy Handsaker, a senior corporate real estate manager for the Colorado-based engineering firm CH2M Hill (CH), a Fortune 500 company with $7 billion USD in 2012 revenue, said, "By not committing to a multi-market, single-source provider exclusively, CH is guaranteed a best-in-class partner for each assignment and avoids having to reinvent the wheel on each transaction."[6]

This shift in thinking and approach underscores the increasingly important role—often driven by rapid advancements in technology—that service providers play in the quality of an end-user's service delivery. Moreover, as the services they deliver become more crucial and carry greater strategic implications, service providers are attempting to transform the perception of what they offer from "what it costs" to what it's actually worth to an end user.

A passage from the 2012 CoreNet Global Corporate Real Estate 2020 report on service delivery and outsourcing elaborates on this premise.

> Service providers are striving to meet end users' demands for strategic global portfolio optimization, workplace mobility, process improvement, energy management, sustainability and cost reduction—all while seeking to shift the value proposition of their services from a cost-based structure to one that pegs success on broader definitions of "value."[7]

End users are responding in kind with their own heightened demands. The above report continues with this:

> CRE executives who want these more diverse and sophisticated services expect true expertise from their providers. A case in point: End users who contract data management services from providers want them to deliver not only data reports but also the kind of in-depth analysis that provides strategic insights.[7]

Disadvantages. Although the multiple-provider model has risen in popularity in recent years, it carries its own inherent disadvantages. The most obvious negative is the increased difficulty and extra labor required to manage multiple providers. While an end user may certainly reap the benefits that come from contracting with a best-in-class provider, it also loses the more integrated, holistic outcome that comes from the single-provider model and is a natural byproduct of more centralized control.

In addition, there is the difficulty of potentially working with multiple technologies and the resulting inconsistent reporting that can occur if the corporate real estate organization does not own the technology platform or require its outsourcing partners to use it. Also, additional internal resources are required to utilize vendor management skills in working with multiple providers.

Hence, the best-in-class aspect gained from the multiple-service-provider model may offset, at least in part, inefficiencies arising from those providers performing in their own spheres and not operating as part of a larger whole.

In a May 2012 *Professional Outsourcing* article titled "Multi-Sourcing or Bundled Services? An Answer to the Riddle," the author affirmed one advantage of the multiple-provider model while also highlighting a downside:

> Multi-sourcing may well give a client more power and more control over each individual provider, with less dependence on each. However, increased control comes at a price in terms of increased management cost, time, effort and measurement. In multi-provider environments retained management capability needed to manage outsourcing regularly costs between 4–10% of total contract value [*and higher for offshored outsourcing*].[8]

Integrator Model

A third outsourcing model has arisen that plays on some of the strengths of the multiple provider model while addressing some of its weaknesses: the integrated approach, which is also known as the integrator model. The integrator model can apply to both facilities management and corporate real estate services, and in fact has been the longtime industry norm in facilities management. For many years, a single firm has been given the responsibility of delivering facilities management; in response, that firm would contract with best-in-class local providers to deliver a comprehensive solution managed by a single vendor.

In more recent years, corporate real estate professionals have begun to use the integrator model, contracting with a single outsource partner to select and manage different firms to deliver traditional brokerage and project management services that are procured either locally or from a stable of preferred providers within particular regions.

As noted earlier, this hybrid outsourcing model combines the best aspects of both the single- and multiple-service-provider models: best-in-class expertise from multiple providers and centralized control by an umbrella entity known as the integrator. This model may not be a good fit for smaller entities, and only a small number of large global firms have begun to explore this model.

Microsoft is one high-profile end user who adopted this model in 2011 in the wake of what it perceived as serious operational inefficiencies. In a 2012 CoreNet Global report, the software giant outlined—under the heading, *"It's not about cost, it's about performance"*—the challenges that spurred it to implement the integrator model:

- Agreed with our internal clients that we needed to be more strategic;
- Significant operational inconsistency across our operation;
- Huge step forward required for integrated technology platform;
- Lacked consistent access to local provider choice and best in class;
- Inability to measure our performance and prove competitive cost structure; and
- Lacked scalability in FTE (full-time equivalent employee) or provider network.[9]

After adopting the integrator model, the company summarized the positive outcome in this bulleted list:

- Common global platform;

- Managed supplier ecosystem;

- Cross-regional suppliers;

- Local provider choice;

- FTEs spending more time with clients & partners; and

- Center resources subject matter expert (SME) to help.[9]

The integrator model represents a new direction in the evolution of outsourcing, and it provides the end users with another approach to help achieve their goals. The most common objection to this model is that the integrator may be required to oversee the work of competitors, which can prove challenging. Moreover, integrators may have limited ability to bid on the services they are overseeing.

Contract Variations

Within each of the above three models, there are three variations in how services are contracted.

Direct. With this model, the corporate real estate organization holds the contract for individual services and manages the suppliers directly. The organization also makes decisions on whether to subcontract certain services or handle them internally.

Managing agent. In this case, the service provider manages the subcontracts on behalf of the corporate real estate organization and owns the relationship and pricing with subcontractors as part of the service delivery model. Either the corporate real estate organization or the service provider can make decisions about whether tasks will be subcontracted depending on the established governance.

Principal. In this type of contract, the corporate real estate organization manages the service provider performing the services, while the service provider determines if it will perform certain services or subcontract at its own discretion.

Contract Pricing

"At-Risk" Compensation

To highlight the growing importance of service-provider performance to a company's bottom-line value proposition to its clients, the majority of outsourcing contracts today include an "at-risk" component of overall compensation. This is also in response to a movement away from fixed-price contracts toward performance-based, or gainshare contracts.

According to the 2013 outsourcing report from Deloitte and CoreNet Global, 73% of buyers surveyed put a portion of service-provider compensation on the line, "if the balanced scorecard targets are not hit, as well as using management fee incentives or shared savings if targets are surpassed."[2]

Typically, a company will conduct quarterly performance reviews to determine if targets are being met, a practice that encourages service providers to stretch and exercise their innovative muscles. For instance, a service provider supplying facilities management services might develop a new power-saving technology that results in utility savings beyond the stated target. In such a case, the vendor might, in fact, be rewarded with a share of those savings.

In addition to the use of balanced scorecards, a strong governance structure is required to monitor performance, as is having good baseline and KPI (key performance indicators) data to track performance improvements.[3] It makes sense for companies to focus on key performance indicators that have the most impact on their business. Fewer, more meaningful indicators have been proven to drive greater enterprise value than multiple, less-strategically focused key performance indicators.

Competitive Bids

Given the competitive pressures of the contemporary marketplace, organizations do not simply monitor their current providers' performance. As noted in the KPMG survey, instead of just routinely renewing the provider's existing contract, organizations commonly seek bids from other providers.[3] The request for proposal process, which can span several quarters, will typically require signficant investment from the organization and its service providers and will often involve specialized consultants hired specifically for the purpose. As the report explains,

> The goal is to test the waters of the market and understand what differentiated services alternative providers could potentially offer, as well as ensure that buyers are getting the best price available for the services in scope and are best leveraging the current capabilities in the market.[3]

The Future of Outsourcing

Outsourcing is now an established part of corporate real estate service delivery for many companies, and it is growing. As revealed in the 2014 KPMG Global Real Estate & Facilities Management Outsourcing Pulse survey, 36% of occupiers reported plans to increase outsourcing during the next 1-2 quarters. Sixty-four percent planned to increase outsourcing during the next 3-4 quarters, and 75 percent planned to increase outsourcing over the following year or longer.[1]

A Final Point

One of the most important factors in achieving an efficient and successful outsourcing initiative is change management. A company considering a major outsourcing initiative should include a detailed change-management program as part of the outsourcing. This process could involve many disciplines within the outsourcing company—from HR and finance to core business operations. A detailed change-management plan—which sets and manages expectations for everyone within the organization—can help ensure a successful outcome.

References

1. Bouri, G., Acoba, F., and Wu, P. (2008, July/August). Organizational Design: Leading Practice Considerations for Corporate Real Estate. *The Leader,* pp. 14–24. Retrieved from https://resources.corenetglobal.org/knowledgecenteronline/SearchByTopicAndResource.aspx?ID=5866

2. Acoba, F., Naudo, C., & James, G. (2013). *Outsourcing: A CoreNet Global and Deloitte Consulting research project.* Retrieved from https://resources.corenetglobal.org/knowledgecenteronline/SearchByTopicAndResource.aspx?ID=3647

3. KPMG. (2013). *KPMG 2013 Global real estate & facilities management (REFM) outsourcing pulse survey.* Retrieved from https://resources.corenetglobal.org/knowledgecenteronline/SearchByTopicAndResource.aspx?ID=749

4. Cushman & Wakefield. (2013). *Global Trends in Real Estate Outsourcing, 2012-2013.* Retrieved from http://annualreview.cushwake.com/downloads/03_global_trends_RE.pdf

5. Brister, K., Layda, B., & Ochalla K. (2012, July/August). Service delivery and outsourcing: Strategic alignment of the external resource network. *The Leader,* 42–45. Retrieved from https://resources.corenetglobal.org/knowledgecenteronline/SearchByTopicAndResource.aspx?ID=4362

6. Steuber, S. D., & Simpson, T. (2014, March/April). The polygamy of CRE outsourcing. *The Leader,* pp. 22–23. Retrieved from https://resources.corenetglobal.org/knowledgecenteronline/SearchByTopicAndResource.aspx?ID=3172

7. Brister, K., Layda, B., & Ochalla, K. (2012). *CoreNet Global corporate real estate 2020 final report: Service delivery and outsourcing.* Retrieved from https://resources.corenetglobal.org/knowledgecenteronline/SearchByTopicAndResource.aspx?ID=1642

8. Willcocks, L. (2012). Multi-sourcing or bundled services? An answer to the riddle. *Professional Outsourcing Resources.* Retrieved from http://www.professionaloutsourcingmagazine.net/insight/multisourcing-or-bundled-services-an-answer-to-the-riddle

9. *Breaking new ground in CRE in supply chain contracting—Microsoft's global integrator model.* (2012). Report from CoreNet Global Summit, London.

Retrieved from https://resources.corenetglobal.org/knowledgecenteronline/SearchByTopicAndResource.aspx?ID=3777

10. KPMG. (2014). *KPMG 2014 Global real estate & facilities management (REFM) outsourcing pulse survey.* Retrieved from http://www.kpmg-institutes.com/content/dam/kpmg/sharedservicesoutsourcinginstitute/pdf/2015/refm-2014-pulse-report.pdf

Chapter 8

Facility Management

Summary

In chapter 4, which addresses the property life cycle, three phases are identified: acquisition, holding period, and disposition. The holding period, or retention period, is the time the space is held by the corporation, and it is in this phase of the property life cycle that facility management (or facilities management, sometimes abbreviated as FM) comes into play.

Effective facilities management is vital to the success of any organization. At a corporate level, it contributes to the delivery of strategic and operational objectives. On a day-to day level, effective facilities management provides a safe and efficient working environment, which is essential to the performance of any business – whatever its size and scope.[1]

The corporate real estate function, because it often has ultimate responsibility for the entire portfolio, including facilities, and because it typically collaborates with other key functions at a higher level in the corporate hierarchy, is generally regarded as more strategic than facility management, which is more operational in nature. Reporting lines for FM vary, but the function often reports to corporate real estate (e.g., is organized within an overall corporate real estate and facilities organization or department).[2]

"As with many other services, no one tends to notice FM until something goes wrong," observed Information Services Group, a technology insights, market and advisory services company, in a 2012 report.[3]

Generally, it is assumed that corporate real estate is more focused on strategic issues, while facility managers are focused on the day-to-day running of the buildings, reports property and portfolio advisory firm Property Beyond Pty Ltd.[4] Still, gone are the days when a focus on janitorial and engineering services was the primary operating model for most facility managers. More is expected of facility management today, and the stakes have been raised. Not unlike those in corporate real estate, facility management professionals are being challenged to add strategic value to their corporations and to operate at a more strategic level.

What is Facility Management?

The definition of facility management continues to evolve. Following are the definitions used by several facility management organizations:

British Institute of Facilities Management definition: "Facilities management is the integration of processes within an organization to maintain and develop the agreed services which support and improve the effectiveness of its primary activities."[1]

International Facility Management Association (IFMA) definition: "Facility management is a profession that encompasses multiple disciplines to ensure functionality of the built environment by integrating people, place and technology."[5]

South Africa Facilities Management Association definition: "Facilities Management is an enabler of sustainable enterprise performance through the whole life management of productive workplaces and effective business support services."[6]

Facility management services are often categorized as either "hard" services or "soft" services. "Hard" services include electrical, mechanical, electro-mechanical, water management, fire safety system maintenance, and energy management. "Soft" services include housekeeping (e.g., janitorial), catering, security, horticulture and landscaping, transportation, health and safety, and mailroom.[7]

A more detailed list of facility management services – in this case those provided by a large, global real estate service provider organization – illustrates the scope of facility management today:[8]

- Critical systems management

- Sustainability programs

- Energy management and procurement
- Emergency preparedness / business continuity planning
- Proactive / predictive maintenance
- Engineering and maintenance services (mobile)
- Housekeeping and janitorial services
- Moves, adds and changes
- Vendor management and rationalization
- Catering and hospitality services
- Vendor contract administration
- Compliance and regulatory management
- Environment, health and safety
- Business support services
- Fleet management
- Security services

Service Delivery for Facility Management

As discussed in chapter 7, most large global corporations deploy a service-delivery model for corporate real estate that includes an internal real estate department supported by external real estate service providers. Facility management is among the top three most frequently outsourced real estate functions.[9]

Within the broad category of facility management, the most commonly outsourced area is workplace services. This includes activities such as janitorial, cafeteria, and amenities services. Sixty-nine percent of organizations responding to a 2014 KPMG survey have already fully outsourced workplace services, 27 percent have partially outsourced them, and just 2 percent have no plans to outsource this type of work. The second most frequently outsourced area of facility management is facilities services (e.g., HVAC, electrical, mechanical, building repair). These activities are fully or partially outsourced by 86 percent of survey respondents, with just 6 percent having no plans to outsource these activities.[10]

A 2014 CoreNet Global survey revealed that placing fees at risk (32%), performance incentives (28%) and shared savings (14%) were the top three "levers" occupiers are using to drive desired behavior among FM suppliers.[11]

That survey also asked occupiers about their key performance indicators (e.g., KPIs) for facility management. Some of the most frequently cited KPIs included:

- Customer satisfaction

- Response time

- Waste reduction

- Cost per square foot / meter

- Financial management

- Quality of work

- Performance (current versus historical)

- Team collaboration

- Complaints

- Level of staffing turnover

According to the Information Services Group report, the best way to ensure mutual accountability is for the end-user client and service provider teams to have the same sets of critical and key performance indicators.[3] Examples could include:

- No more than 5% of non-urgent work orders delayed by more than 24 hours

- 97% of delayed work orders resolved within 24 hours

- 97% uptime of non-critical space

- 99.9% uptime of critical space (e.g. data centers, executive offices)

- Above average grades in customer surveys

While important to any outsourcing relationship, ongoing communication and attention to detail are particularly crucial to facilities management. In a human resources or finance outsourcing arrangement, for instance, internal customers deal with service providers on a relatively infrequent basis, and interactions typically involve specific tasks or functions. Services delivered by a facilities provider, however, impact all of a client's employees on a daily basis, and involve multiple points of potential failure. If someone spills something in a lobby, if a parking lot isn't cleared of snow, if offices are too hot or too cold, or if restrooms are dirty, the facilities management service provider is accountable.[3]

Operation and Maintenance

Facilities are living, if not breathing, structures requiring ongoing care and maintenance. If they are well maintained, they are business assets; if they are neglected, they can become liabilities. At the same time a building's health is sustained, customer demands must be addressed, ever-changing regulatory codes must be met with modifications to ensure compliance, and paperwork must be filed. But these are not inexpensive propositions, and limited budgets tend to favor business initiatives that are more immediately apparent to stakeholders.

Facility managers, then, often must do more with less to preserve the building's functionality and value while meeting the company's brand and regulatory requirements. They understand that fines for being out of compliance, which are often easily avoidable, add up quickly.

One suggested approach to this challenge is to engage in what might be called the "Herzberg method" of building maintenance. This method is based on the theories of motivation by renowned psychologist Frederick Herzberg. In facility-management terms, Herzberg's 1959 "Two Factor Theory of Motivation" holds that increasing workplace satisfaction requires a focus on the nature of employees' work, while reducing dissatisfaction requires a focus on the workplace itself, including the hygiene of the built environment.[12]

This theory has led to a theoretical basis of workplace service levels coined by Simon Wilson of Cushman & Wakefield and Mike Dawson of Nokia Workplace Resources. Their approach suggests providing a "baseline experience" to building-maintenance services, then measuring correlations between the experience levels and employee satisfaction. The result is a cost-effective, minimum level of service that addresses building-specific standards without overextending the budget or doing more than necessary to keep employees satisfied.[13]

Beyond building hygiene as a building-satisfaction factor lies the enormous issue of occupancy comfort. The two main components of comfort—lighting, and heating and air conditioning solutions—account for the largest expenses in operations and maintenance for any building. They represent as much as 70% of energy-related costs, according to the U.S. Department of Energy.[14]

To reduce these costs, manufacturers of lighting and heating, ventilation and air conditioning (HVAC) solutions regularly introduce new technologies such as application-specific controls or intelligent, whole-building systems that can be choreographed according to building occupancy schedules or production factors. These systems are often supplemented with reporting functions—energy analysis, system-fault diagnosis, carbon-footprint measurements, etc.—to validate the energy savings that are achievable.[15]

Leading Trends and Issues

The 2014 CoreNet Global survey on facilities management revealed that cost reduction (cited by 73% of respondents), enhancing the employee experience (68%), and standardization and consolidation (58%) were the top three priorities for their facility management service delivery strategy.

"There has never been the emphasis on cost that there is now and facility managers, to be successful, must realize that fact," states the *Facility Management Handbook*, Third Edition, published in 2010.[16] "There is an unrelenting cost squeeze on facility departments."

Other observations on the state of facility management from the *Facility Management Handbook* include:

- The function and the facility manager still are not viewed as important within the company as, for example, Human Resources or Information Technology, and their managers.

- Facility managers generally do not have the knowledge or expertise of a business leader.

- The predicted personnel crunch has arrived as "baby boomers" retire from management, supervisory and technical positions.

- Areas in which FM operates (the built environment, utilities, safety, etc.) are increasingly being regulated by all levels of government.

- Energy to run facilities has become a major cost, and an even greater public relations issue.

In addition, the *Handbook* authors state, "you only need to monitor the recent issues of facility management trade publications to recognize the importance of sustainability. We suspect that any facility manager who does not have the topic high on his agenda will have it placed there by customers."

The Importance of Demonstrating Value

For years, facility management thought leaders have worked to identify ways to better demonstrate the value of facility management. In a 2012 global forum on the issue, the majority of participants ranked focusing on productivity, revenue, and cost control as the key to changing or raising the status of facility management in the eyes of business leaders. Other means for instigating change, participants agreed, are complying with facility codes, showing expertise for the job, and satisfying resident employees with regard to their workplace environment.[17]

At a 2012 CoreNet Global Summit, members of the association's Strategic Facilities Management Knowledge Community identified at least three specific ways that facility management adds value to the overall organization:

1. To the corporation as a whole, facility management brings "quality management of standards and processes in the daily management of facilities."

2. To the business units, facility management serves as a reliable knowledge base and the source of solutions that meet the tangible needs of the occupants of specific buildings.

3. To company employees, facility management serves as a reliable service entity that maintains a pleasant and productive place to work, thereby promoting employee engagement and a positive company brand.[18]

Conclusion

Ask the average worker in any office or on any manufacturing floor about the role of a facility manager and you likely will hear that the facility manager keeps the lights on and the heating and air conditioning system in working order, maintains the landscaping, and sees to it that janitorial and building-aesthetics services are conducted according to each company's standards and budget.

But there is much more to facility management. It not only provides a safe, efficient working environment, it contributes to the delivery of corporate strategic and operational objectives. A key challenge for facility management is to continue documenting and communicating its value proposition.

References

1. British Institute of Facilities Management. Retrieved from http://www.bifm.org.uk/bifm/about/facilities

2. CoreNet Global London Summit. (2012, September). Presentation. Raising the Bar: Enhancing the Strategic Role of Facilities Management. Retrieved from https://resources.corenetglobal.org/knowledgecenteronline/SearchByTopicAndResource.aspx?ID=1159

3. Information Services Group (ISG). (2012). *Facilities Management Outsourcing: Prioritizing Activities is Critical to Success.* Retrieved from http://www.isg-one.com/knowledgecenter/whitepapers/private/papers/White_paper_-_Facilities-Management-Outsourcing.pdf

4. Property Beyond Pty Ltd. Retrieved from http://www.propertybeyond.com.au/publications/84-blank

5. International Facility Management Association. Retrieved from http://www.ifma.org/know-base/browse/what-is-fm-

6. South Africa Facilities Management Association. Retrieved from http://www.safma.co.za/portals/0/What_is_FM_presentation.pdf

7. Service Futures. Retrieved from http://servicefutures.com/facility-management/state-fm-today/

8. Cushman & Wakefield. Retrieved from http://www.cushmanwakefield.com/en/services/facilities-management/

9. KPMG. (2013). *KPMG 2013 Global real estate & facilities management (REFM) outsourcing pulse survey.* Retrieved from https://resources.corenetglobal.org/knowledgecenteronline/SearchByTopicAndResource.aspx?ID=749

10. KPMG. (2014). *KPMG 2014 Global real estate & facilities management (REFM) outsourcing pulse survey.* Retrieved from http://www.kpmg-institutes.com/content/dam/kpmg/sharedservicesoutsourcinginstitute/pdf/2015/refm-2014-pulse-report.pdf

11. CoreNet Global. (2014). Facilities Management Survey results. Retrieved from https://resources.corenetglobal.org/knowledgecenteronline/SearchByTopicAndResource.aspx?ID=6597

12. Boundless. (2014, November). *Herzberg's two-factor theory.* Retrieved from https://www.boundless.com/business/textbooks/boundless-business-textbook/motivation-theories-and-applications-11/theories-on-motivation-75/herzberg-s-two-factor-theory-357-1146/

13. Dawson, M., & Wilson, S. (2011, September). *Workplace experience levels: Putting the human equation back into global facilities management.* Presentation at CoreNet Global Summit 2011, Paris.

14. Hall, C., & Maldeis, N. (2014). Benefits of integrating lighting and HVAC controls. *Today's Facility Manager*. Retrieved from http://todaysfacilitymanager.com/2014/10/benefits-of-integrating-lighting-and-hvac-controls/

15. Reiser, K., & Probst, D. (2012, April/May). *Driving unprecedented efficiency and productivity gains with smart technology and facility management.* Presentation at CoreNet Global Summit 2012, San Diego, CA.

16. Cotts, David G., Roper, Kathy O., and Payant, Richard P. (2010). *Facility Management Handbook.* 3rd Edition. Published by American Management Association. New York.

17. Varcoe, D. B., Hicks, J., & Zurich CRE & FM Team. (2012, June). *CRE & FM futures forum final report.* Fareham, Hampshire, UK: Zurich Insurance Group. Retrieved from https://resources.corenetglobal.org/knowledgecenteronline/SearchByTopicAndResource.aspx?ID=5680

18. CoreNet Global. (2012, October). *Strategic facilities management community report.* Orlando, FL.

Chapter 9

Performance Management

Summary

For decades, the financial, manufacturing, and professional services industries have measured performance, conducted routine analysis, and monitored trends to inform decisions and drive improvements in operational and financial results. Now, corporate real estate executives are responding to calls to improve performance, do more with less, and advance strategic decision-making by leveraging newly available tools, including meaningful benchmarking, for performance management.

Clearly defining desired business outcomes is critical to the success of a performance management strategy. Organizations need to thoughtfully determine which business results matter the most so they can select and report on key performance indicators that ensure and measure achievement and anticipate internal and external benchmarking. In addition, key performance indicators are a useful tool to communicate results and opportunities in a meaningful and succinct way to executive management.

Comprehensive Performance Management Plan

Corporate real estate professionals need a comprehensive performance management program in order to demonstrate that corporate real estate is a top-tier support function in their organization. A strong program allows executives to meet economic challenges by ensuring they are more effectively managing corporate spending and delivering strong returns on investment through corporate real estate initiatives, regardless of market or geography.

A broader range of cost-effective options for efficient and accurate data collection and tools for robust analytics have become more widely available in recent years. These options provide the corporate real estate professionals and the C-suite a new set of tools and insights that can be more easily employed to establish operational, financial, and strategic priorities and to inform executive decision-making and goal setting.

According to *Understanding Business Performance Indicators*, a 2014 survey by CoreNet Global, as many as 95% of corporate real estate professionals report that their organization now relies on a formalized set of performance metrics to make strategic business decisions.[1]

This chapter explains how to implement or enhance a performance management program that will allow the corporate real estate organization to stay competitive in the market. This chapter is divided into three sections with the first defining the approach to performance management, specifically how to choose key performance indicators and how to use them to create internal benchmarks. The second section outlines the process of measuring performance externally against peer organizations and industry standards and benchmarking for service providers. The third section addresses how to analyze, interpret, and communicate results; how to understand reporting costs; and the importance of routine information review and refinement by corporate management. The final section includes a case study that illustrates the process of measuring performance.

How to Create Measurements

The first steps in developing a performance management program are understanding which outcomes matter most to the organization and defining what to measure internally. Several steps are necessary to achieve these goals.

Define Most Important Business Objectives

The corporate real estate organization must know which objectives will contribute the most to the defined corporate outcomes (e.g., reduce portfolio expenses, improve customer satisfaction, expand market share).

It is helpful to engage internal subject matter experts who may lend valuable insights.

Document Critical Success Factors

Decide which factors must be acted upon to achieve the business objectives. For example, if the business objective is to "cut portfolio expenses," the organization may choose several critical success factors such as "identify location consolidation opportunities" or "reduce utilities expenses."

Select Key Performance Indicators

Key performance indicators are measurable data points that demonstrate whether the critical success factors are being accomplished. Continuing with the prior example, if the critical success factor is "reduce utilities costs," one key performance indicator selected could be energy consumption per month. When selecting key performance indicators, it is important to include lagging (backward-looking) and leading (forward-looking) indicators as well as subjective and objective measures of performance.

Table 9.1 provides another example of this process, using a common business objective: improving customer experience.

Objective	Critical Success Factor	Key Performance Indicators
Improve the customer experience	Ensure service requests are handled quickly and accurately	Average completion time of service requests Percentage of total requests that are repeats
	Survey customers on their experience	Customer satisfaction survey results

Table 9.1. Selecting Key Performance Indicators

Each corporate real estate organization has its own particular market and business goals that should be reflected in its choice of key performance indicators. For example, cost-driven, task-oriented corporate real estate companies may focus more heavily on space utilization and facility management metrics, while a more strategic organization will define metrics based on company strategy. Furthermore, determining the desired level of tracking involves balancing the resources required to capture and report on the key performance indicators against the value of expected results.

In the 2014 CoreNet Global *Understanding Business Performance Indicators* survey, as many as 79% of respondents said their organization has a formal process of gathering key performance indicators data, and more than half of the respondents also said that key performance indicators or other performance metrics are viewed by their senior management and C-suite executives as fundamental to making informed, strategic decisions.[1]

The following key performance indicators are among those most commonly identified by corporate real estate organizations, according to the CoreNet Global survey.[1]

Real estate costs. Upfront costs to build and recurring costs to maintain space for employees and operations are often calculated in cost per unit, cost per workspace or cost per full-time employee equivalent. More than 89% of survey respondents said their organization identifies costs as a key performance indicator.[1]

Space / utilization. This indicator measures the use of existing assets, such as square feet / meters per employee, occupancy and vacancy rates, and actual use of space. As many as 88% of survey respondents said space / utilization is a key indicator for their organization.[1]

Customer satisfaction. The perceived value of the corporate real estate organization is measured throughout its own enterprise regarding satisfaction of customers and clients of the core business. Fifty-five percent of respondents said customer satisfaction is one of their organization's key performance indicators.[1]

Other popular categories of key performance indicators include revenue and margin improvements, operations, efficiency, corporate social responsibility, and employee productivity.

Report Key Performance Indicators

Once the indicators have been selected, it is critical to understand how each measure is calculated, where data will be captured, and how associated reports will be generated (format, frequency, distribution, etc.). This may require establishing new work processes to ensure data can be collected in the most timely and accurate way possible.

As the reporting is being developed, it is advisable to review results internally to ensure that they are accurate and that the data is valid and not easily manipulated. Be prepared to fine-tune or even dramatically modify key performance indicators or required business processes before distributing them fully.

When these new reports are distributed, it is critical that the users clearly understand how to interpret the results and how to use them to identify steps to positively impact a key performance indicator. A useful approach is to create a simple guide that includes screenshots of the report, highlighting areas that need specific focus or action, and providing simple instructions on what to do if results are above or below target.

Establish Internal Benchmarking

Once the initial reporting is in place, the results should be analyzed to determine baseline performance for each facility and facility function in business units for the entire enterprise. That baseline then is used to establish the internal benchmark, which serves as the starting point for setting goals. Understanding this starting point is critical to understanding the organization's strengths and weaknesses and knowing where to focus efforts to promote cost management and improve performance. While this internal data can eventually be benchmarked externally, internal evaluation can often produce greater results initially because anomalies can be more thoroughly analyzed, understood, and adjusted for variations. Internal benchmarking should be layered—one step building on the next—and follow a prescribed two-step path.

Track a single facility over time. This type of analysis can include key performance indicators such as costs per square foot / meter, square footage / meters per person / seat, and utilization and vacancy rates, which can provide valuable insight into how a facility is being managed relative to demand for goods and services.

Compare equivalent facility functions within a single business unit. After a single facility has been tracked over time, these metrics can be used to compare an organization's equivalent facilities to each other, even if there are geographic differences. For example, labor costs and market rental rates per square foot in New York City will be higher than those in Atlanta for comparable types of office space. However, understanding the market rates between the two cities can allow for cost adjustments.

It is important to evaluate results over time to identify trends and anomalies and uncover the reasons leading to certain patterns (e.g., cyclical variation, new business line, major turnover, etc.), in order to track improvements or address issues.

Measure Across Units

Internal benchmarking is sometimes confined to one business unit as it may not always be valid across multiple disparate groups. For example, an industrial business would not benchmark well in certain asset classes or locations with a business unit in the financial sector. However, benchmarking across business units can serve to identify best practices and can serve as a motivational tool to prompt lagging units to improve their real estate results. Such facilities as general office space, data centers, and call centers can be successfully benchmarked across multiple business units.

External Benchmarking

When an enterprise can accurately measure its own data over time, it is ready to benchmark itself against peer organizations and wider industry standards. New technologies and data aggregation and normalization techniques now facilitate external benchmarking. While this technique is growing in popularity, only about 39% of respondents in the 2014 CoreNet Global *Understanding Business Performance Indicators* survey said they benchmark real estate key performance indicators against other organizations.[1] However, when performed correctly, external benchmarking can significantly advance a company's performance improvement agenda.

Additionally, the same performance measurement principles that apply to internal and external evaluations can also be applied to service provider evaluations. Just as corporate real estate organizations want their employees and existing portfolio to achieve a high level of performance, they should expect the same from their service providers.

Industry and Peer Benchmarking

To further improve internal performance, external benchmarking is often initiated by the C-suite to identify areas of opportunity related to cost and quality of service as well as to gauge how effectively a portfolio is being managed. In an era of "big data" and associated analytics, corporate executives routinely apply metrics to identify patterns, trends, and anomalies in their core businesses. Sophisticated mathematical models and the use of algorithms are used routinely in most businesses in pursuit of continuous improvement.

When benchmarking performance with external data sources—including from among an organization's peers, industry, types of uses, geographies, form of tenancy / ownership—it is a common practice to examine metrics in the following three categories to account for demand-side variability.

Business function. These metrics are applicable among businesses that produce similar goods and services. Revenue per square foot / meter or total occupancy cost per unit are valid business-to-business functional comparisons because they account for strategic decisions.

Organizational function. While each space has different requirements for technology, security, workplace utilization, and more, comparisons of organizational function can be made based on similar use within an organization, including individual groups such as accounting, software development, engineering, customer service, and sales.

Facility. By filtering for type of facility, geography, ownership / lease type, currency, and occupancy levels, real estate executives can accurately benchmark with other companies. Generally, facilities such as retail stores, call centers, distribution centers, and data centers, for example, should be compared only against their own facility type, though mixed-use facilities can also be benchmarked given a standardized data normalization methodology.

When benchmarking externally, it's important to ensure that the comparisons are valid and that the items used in the analyses are commensurable—as described in the three categories detailed above. Benchmarking *across* property types, geographies, asset classes, forms of occupant, and other factors can be accomplished when adding a time dimension to the data collection.

Other Forms of Benchmarking

Once an organization flexes its performance management muscles, corporate real estate executives may wish to utilize these newly mastered skills for improving management of contractual relationships, including those with service provider partners. Principles developed for benchmarking can be leveraged to better measure the performance of third-party vendors or other service providers.

When facility management service providers work onsite or when the scale and significance of facility management or real estate transaction spending is relevant, a balanced scorecard can be a useful tool. Such a process can ensure results align to expectations, focus is placed on the right actions, and improvement opportunities are identified. Metrics in two categories are often used.

Functional quantitative metrics. Standard categories may be used, but individual business units may define metrics particular to their needs. Examples include:

- Cost, quality, and response time

- Health and safety

- Business continuity and risk management

Qualitative and relationship metrics. These offer support for activities outside of a statement of work. These include:

- Service orientation

- Overall alliance behavior

- Technological leadership

- Early supplier involvement in initiatives / projects

- Continuous improvement

- Customer satisfaction

A balanced scorecard will ensure that a wide range of objectives are addressed and that one area is not sacrificed for the benefit of another. For example, if all of the key performance indicators were the cost measures, a service provider's success at customer satisfaction would likely decline, detracting from the corporate real estate team's long-term ability to influence decisions and create value for the enterprise.

When tailored to the specific needs and developed in partnership with the corporate real estate service provider, this scorecard can help achieve buy-in, improve the organization's ability to monitor the provider's performance and drive positive change and desired behaviors.

Evaluation of Measurements

As with any business improvement effort, it is not enough to merely measure and internally analyze performance metrics. In order to deliver tangible improvements, the information must be made actionable and then communicated throughout the relevant business units.

An organization that cascades performance results and associated action plans to its employees and partners and applies the lessons learned from its own benchmarking to its wider sphere of business relationships will ensure that performance management will yield broader, sustained, operational improvements.

Furthermore, organizations committed to real growth and performance analysis will understand that there is a cost to implementing and maintaining these internal processes and realize they must be evaluated on a regular basis to ensure they are continually relevant—especially as the business goals evolve and change over time. Challenges that must be considered when establishing a performance management program include the cost of data collection and reporting as well as ensuring the integrity of the data collected.

Communicating the Results

Communicating the results of corporate real estate performance measurements beyond the C-suite, whether internally or externally generated, is vital to ensuring that the maximum value is gained from the performance management program.

Communication can be accomplished in a variety of ways. These include formal monthly, quarterly, or annual reports with "user-definable" charts and other summaries, comprehensive, real-time performance dashboards, and full-length reports explaining the results. Firms are increasingly delivering performance results in internal publications, on company intranet sites, and directly on dashboards within the relevant departments.

Of the respondents in the CoreNet Global 2014 *Understanding Business Performance Indicators* survey, 66% communicate key performance indicators and other metrics through formal reports and 56% by dashboard. A little over 14% reported using the company's intranet site to communicate performance data.[1]

Regardless of the method, the key to effectively communicating performance results is understanding the audience and disseminating targeted information clearly. Organizations often make the mistake of overloading readers with too many statistics and data, so it is important to focus on sharing the select key performance indicators that provide a full view of the group's performance.

Cost of Measuring

It is important to take into account the time and resource implications of data collection and reporting. Depending on the resources available in the corporate real estate organization, this job can range from a part-time effort to a full-time responsibility for employees in a variety of positions.

Nearly half of the respondents in the CoreNet Global 2014 *Understanding Business Performance Indicators* survey reported that the organization's finance group is responsible for collecting and tracking key performance indicators and other performance metrics, while 30% said their shared services groups do the job, 21% named HR as responsible, and 10% said their organization's IT department collects performance data.[1]

Data Integrity

A common challenge to measuring performance is the consistency and integrity of the data. Corporate real estate performance metrics are typically collected by in-house personnel, and it is common for the accuracy of the data to be questioned by those collecting it or evaluating the results. Third-party aggregation and normalization from a trusted and independent resource can do much to head off the predictable questions that will arise concerning the accuracy of the data.

Just 30% of respondents in a 2012 study conducted by CoreNet Global and Deloitte Consulting LLP completely trusted their own performance management data (slide 21).[2] It is therefore important to clearly communicate at the outset how each measure is calculated, the source of the data, and any exclusions from the data set. Individuals with direct responsibility for business processes that drive key performance indicators should be able to capably address data accuracy and affirm the validity or directional correctness of reported results.

Regular Review

Each corporate real estate organization must decide how often performance metrics should be reported, and that frequency may be based on a number of organizational factors, including corporate planning and business cycles. Almost half (45%) of respondents in the CoreNet Global 2014 *Understanding Business Performance Indicators* survey said their organizations review performance measurements quarterly, while 39% of respondents review them monthly.[1] Real-time reporting is also increasingly available to management.

But, as with any business improvement process, regular review and evaluation are critical to the ultimate goal of improving outcomes. Organizations are dynamic, and whatever metrics are measured should be reviewed periodically, checked, and challenged to ensure that the corporate real estate organization remains aligned and relevant to its ever-evolving business needs and strategies.

Pitfalls to Avoid

Common pitfalls to avoid when first establishing a performance measurement program include selecting metrics that do not support the overarching business objectives, choosing too many metrics, setting overly aggressive targets, responding poorly to missing target performance and overburdening the limited staff typically tasked with reporting. Performance management is a forward-thinking and proven methodology to help organizations make better decisions and achieve better results. Performance management works best when it is an embedded part of corporate culture across the entire enterprise.

Case Study

Office Space Example

Is it cost per full-time equivalent or space utilization that is driving my numbers?

A CoreNet Global member participating in the association's benchmarking system ran a report comparing cost per full-time equivalent for office space in a target geography and discovered the organization was operating at the high end of the range, both within and outside its industry peer group. An example of the report follows in Figure 9.2, showing an average of $9,377 USD and a wide range of outcomes—from under $6,000 USD per full-time equivalent to over $12,000 USD.

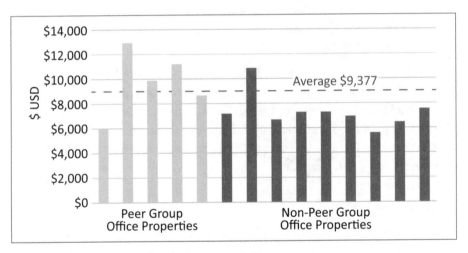

Figure 9.2. Office Space Cost per Full-Time Equivalent

In the graph, the yellow bars represent the company's own industry peer group while the green bars represent a different peer group of office users that they examined to augment the comparison set. The chart represents cost per full-time equivalent for office properties, and the system allowed the member to select for geography, exclude the impact of virtual employees, and eliminate surplus properties.

By reviewing the individual data points, the member was able not only to identify its cost versus the average—which is how most benchmarking comparisons are done—but also to identify the range of individual values. By way of example, a real estate executive using the above chart would quickly observe a large clustering in the $6,000 to $7,000 USD range, indicating that the company's above-average performance reflects a meaningful opportunity, not an opportunity distorted by the presence of a few outlying values. Additionally, the member analyzed report data showing:

- Square feet /meters per seat
- Number of full-time equivalents per seat
- Cost per square foot / meter

For instance, the square feet-per-seat metric ranged from 180 to about 320, with the client coming in close to 240.

The participant learned that its cost per square foot for office space was higher than its industry peers, which in turn drove an opportunity to reduce its high occupancy costs vis-à-vis the peer group and other office users. However, because its cost profile of owned versus leased properties differed, the real estate team needed to differentiate the company's cost profile by ownership type and so prepared a targeted report revealing detailed cost metrics for owned-versus-leased office properties within the study area location.

A review of data relative to owned properties resulted in the conclusion that the company's property depreciation was higher than that among the peer group companies—a fact reflecting a series of recent, high-cost investments in new facilities. The team also learned that their operating expenses—which are more controllable—were actually fully in line if not somewhat better than that among the peer group, possibly as a result of capital investments. The senior corporate real estate executive recognized that investment decisions led to a higher general and administrative cost profile and that there were more productive initiatives than pursuing aggressive cost management initiatives in the owned-property portfolio.

Conclusion

Every corporate real estate organization can be placed along a continuum of maturity in its application of performance management techniques, just as every business faces its own set of challenges, goals, and objectives. A corporate real estate organization's performance management is a tool in delivering superior service and costs to its internal customers in conformance with broad operational and financial objectives. Selecting appropriate metrics and key indicators for reporting performance within the organization, performing external benchmarking against peer organizations and industries, and communicating the results internally and externally should be goals. The objective of a performance measurement program should be constructive, with the ultimate goal of identifying and solving performance problems and experiencing continuous improvement for all facets of the corporate real estate organization.

Ultimately, performance management will be a key hallmark of an organization as it builds and implements a roadmap to a better align a real estate strategy with the strategy of the core business.

References

1. CoreNet Global. (2014). *Understanding business performance indicators.* Retrieved from https://resources.corenetglobal.org/knowledgecenteronline/SearchByTopicAndResource.aspx?ID=5932

2. CoreNet Global and Deloitte Consulting LLP. (2012, July). Performance management survey results. Retrieved from https://resources.corenetglobal.org/knowledgecenteronline/SearchByTopicAndResource.aspx?ID=2240

Chapter 10

Corporate Real Estate Technology

Summary

Corporate real estate professionals depend heavily on technology tools to manage complex real estate portfolios. In many cases, those portfolios comprise millions of square feet / meters of space and hundreds, perhaps even thousands of individual locations around the world. The need for a robust technology platform to manage these real property assets is obvious.

To be sure, there are a lot of options. A recent study by CoreTEch, the corporate real estate technology focus within RealComm (e.g., a worldwide research and event company focused on the intersection of technology, innovation and real estate operations) cited more than 750 real estate applications in the market.[1]

Software tools to manage corporate real estate generally fall into one of three categories:

1. Single Point systems (i.e., generally separate database repositories designed to service a single element of the real estate life cycle, such as lease management or facility management).

2. Enterprise Resource Planning (ERP) systems. ERP software is typically a suite of integrated applications that are used to collect, store, manage and interpret data from a wide range of business activities. Some of the larger ERP system companies offer modules to manage elements of corporate real estate.

3. Integrated Workplace Management systems, or IWMS (i.e., generally providing the opportunity to select individual components or a suite of integrated functionality with a common database structure). IWMS offerings typically include portfolio management, project management, facilities management, occupancy management, and environmental sustainability.[1]

Each of these options has strengths and weaknesses. Companies make different choices based on a variety of factors: cost, risk, legacy systems, preferences of senior management, platforms available through their real estate service provider organizations, and more. (Several large global real estate service provider companies have developed technology platforms to serve their corporate real estate clients.)

In addition, Computer-Aided Facilities Management (CAFM) software is available to support operational and strategic facility management.

This chapter is devoted to a discussion of the three options listed above, with emphasis on IWMS.

Single Point Systems

Single Point systems focus on a single area of service, such as Facility Management or Portfolio Management. They provide strong functionality in that area, and implementation is straightforward since there are no cross-functional activities. This combination of strong functionality and simple implementation makes Single Point systems an attractive option for many companies.[1]

The tradeoff is that multiple systems must be purchased and supported, with different training required for each. There is no data sharing, no leveraging of analytics, and no way to consolidate the information and report up without additional expenditures for a data warehouse that integrates all the systems, and for a reporting engine.

Single Point systems or solutions can be a good choice for smaller companies, or companies which have outsourced a significant amount of their real estate operations to service providers. They also may be appropriate for companies with a decentralized or distributed organizational model in which there is little need or pressure to share data.

Enterprise Resource Planning (ERP) Systems

In their quest to organize around a single technology system for all their major business functions, some companies prefer to use the corporate ERP system for real estate management. This is a conceptually plausible approach. Yet some observers have noted that current ERP systems are primarily financial systems and thus cannot handle all of the day-to-day operational functions required to manage a large, complex real estate portfolio. This can lead to additional programming and customization costs, and sometimes employees will create so-called "shadow" systems (i.e., in spreadsheets) to address the gap in capabilities.[1]

Still, prudent corporate real estate professionals will recognize the value that the enterprise places on leveraging its ERP solution, even if the real estate module of that ERP solution does not offer the functionality and transparency of operation they want when compared to other real estate applications. If senior management places a premium on having a single enterprise-wide system of record for all financial and operational information, this consideration may prevail.[2]

Integrated Workplace Management Systems (IWMS)

Integrated workplace management systems are sometimes referred to as the "total package" because they include all the functionality required throughout the entire real estate life cycle.[1] Since IWMS has an integrated database, users do not have to contend with having the same portfolio data located in multiple systems (as is the case with Single Point solutions), nor do they need to create "shadow" systems to fill the voids that can occur when using ERP systems for operational activities.

Integrated workplace management systems represent today's state of the art in technology platforms for corporate real estate management. Implementation of an IWMS, however, can be complex.[3] In addition, these systems can be costly.[4]

Nine previously distinct disciplines are connected within integrated workplace management systems. These include:

- Real estate / property portfolio management and lease administration

- Site selection

- Transaction management

- Tax management

- Workplace strategic planning

- Capital planning and project management

- Space planning, scheduling, and management

- Operations and maintenance

- Sustainability and energy management

Each of these areas is examined in more depth below.

Real Estate / Property Portfolio Management and Lease Administration

This arena is concerned with the acquisition (both purchase and lease), financial management, administration, and disposition or recycling of corporate real estate property. An integrated workplace management system lets corporate real estate professionals gather data on properties in one place, so they can quickly see:

- Details and location of all property that is owned or leased

- Dates that leases expire or options come due

- Amount paid for each property

- Amount of space allocated in each property

- Amount of space that is being utilized (or underutilized)

- Any income or cost recovery received from leased-out space

New analytic applications can improve decision-making as the real estate strategist can now examine all data on the entire portfolio and see graphic profiles of every property across the globe. This data is critical for a company to understand what is in its portfolio, and it also allows a company to benchmark different properties within its own portfolio and to the market at large. All analysis can be done with the ultimate goal of retaining the right amount and type of space, at the right cost, in the right location, and for the right amount of time.

An integrated workplace management system can analyze the mechanics of a lease, including the tax implications, and even compare and contrast various lease types and financial obligations.

Site Selection

According to research and advisory company Gartner, Inc., "We see a growing need to . . . focus on the complex task of location management before capital project management gets underway. It's important to determine first how to maximize the chances of a proposed facility succeeding in relation to its location."[5] For site selection, integrated workplace management systems must interface with geographic information systems in order to provide all the necessary information for location decisions.

Geographic information systems are most useful for spatially locating one or more properties on a map so that comparisons can be made to data such as utility-provision in the area, workforce in the area, and distance to highways or public transport.

This site selection process also includes asking questions such as:

- Where should we locate our next facility?

- What are the demographics of this region?

- What are the transportation logistics?

- Are there issues regarding the availability of energy?

- What choice of utilities is there, and how much are the associated costs?

- How do we dispose of wastewater?

- Where do our existing employees live in relationship to proposed locations?

- What is the household income or education level around the proposed locations?

Integrated workplace management systems can help determine the answers to those important questions.

Transaction Management

This is the nuts and bolts of buying, selling, and acquiring the use of real property. In this arena, an integrated workplace management system will perform financial analysis of multiple properties, including factors such as rent, required maintenance, term, tenant improvements, and company's cost of capital. Such information can help corporate real estate professionals determine the best options after taking into account both financial and nonfinancial factors (e.g., building quality, staff travel time). Additionally, the system can help manage all the documents involved in the transaction.

Tax Management

Integrated workplace management systems can provide tax management solutions as well, offering the ability to manage multiple types of taxes and value-added provisions from multiple countries and municipalities.

Workplace Strategic Planning

An organization's culture—including its work, branding, community, financial, and employee engagement strategies—needs to align with the built environment to enable peak performance and innovation at the lowest costs. Workplace strategies must be integrated with an organization's business strategies to support the overall goals of the business entity. Integrated workplace management systems provide the key information and planning and analytic tools needed to accomplish these efforts.

Capital Planning and Project Management

These activities are associated with the development and design of new facilities as well as the enhancement, remodeling or reconfiguring of existing ones. Integrated workplace management system features support this discipline through tools that address capital planning, design, funding, bidding, procurement, cost and resource management, project documentation, scheduling, and critical-path analysis.

Project management in integrated workplace management systems can be viewed as both a discipline specific to construction and a way of organizing work into logical, progressive packages where process controls, accountability, and documentation provide rigor. Many of the applications relied on by workplace professionals for project management have been created from the perspective of architects, engineers, or contractors. This can create a serious mismatch, considering that both design and construction are usually outsourced by the owner or operator.

Generally, the owner / operator's role focuses on funding, monitoring, quality control, contract conformance, and related activities, and these activities are often being performed simultaneously on many projects. To aid in this process, integrated workplace management systems provide the ability to structure, view, and manage programs and portfolios of projects that might coordinate or share budgets and resources, and might have timing dependencies. Dashboards serve as important coordination tools, allowing the user to instantly check on the status of projects and programs and to drill into specifics directly and as needed.

The leading integrated workplace management systems can also identify when a project might be needed and enable a methodical, structured review of options. These programs make it easier to take the preferred option through appropriate approvals and funding processes because records that have been created can be taken forward to become the business case for the eventual project and provide the baseline against which its success can be judged.

Space Planning, Scheduling, and Management

These tasks are part of the facility management functions of integrated workplace management systems, which encompass activities related to the operation and optimized utilization of workplaces. The integrated workplace management systems include features that involve the planning and management of space within each building, which are components of the strategic workplace plan.

Computer-aided drawings and building information modeling provide much of the key space data. With that data, integrated workplace management systems can support resource scheduling (e.g., booking of desks, meeting rooms, video conference facilities, and catering) and move management. A good integrated workplace management system will also enable strategic facilities planning (including scenario modeling and analysis), which can identify where space does not match demand.

Not surprisingly, the explosion of mobile computing is increasingly affecting how companies are deploying and using integrated workplace management systems in general and space management systems in particular. Applications are now available on mobile devices that allow space planners in the field to readily refer to drawings and models.

Operations and Maintenance

This facility management function involves corrective, preventive, and predictive maintenance, as well as the ongoing operations of facilities and associated assets, including site and employee service management. Features of integrated workplace management systems that support maintenance management include asset management, work orders/requests, preventive maintenance, work-order administration, warranty tracking, inventory management, vendor management, and facility-condition assessment.

Integrated systems allow organizations to monitor asset conditions so that they can see when preventive maintenance needs to be carried out and understand future financial liabilities for life cycle replacement.

Sustainability and Energy Management

According to the United Nations Environment Program, buildings are estimated to consume as much as 40% of the world's electricity.[6] Measuring and optimizing energy use and waste production (e.g., greenhouse gas emissions, paper, and packaging) within a facility can help improve the sustainable design and management of buildings. Typical integrated workplace management systems support these measures by integrating building management systems, analyzing utilities for billing statements and generation of carbon content calculations, and utilizing sustainability performance metrics, energy benchmarking, carbon-emissions tracking, and waste-stream tracking.

In some packages, energy-efficiency project analysis is aided here with an interface to building information modeling, which can display various sustainable design alternatives for new buildings or renovations. Other tools may include the ability to review data about an existing building and identify energy efficiency projects along with the supporting business case.

Benefits of Integration

Some of the benefits provided by an integrated workplace management system include:

- A single view of the "truth," as all portfolio data is in one place and not repeated across multiple systems;

- Holistic data about a property/portfolio gathered in one place spanning all nine areas discussed previously;

- Improved ability to make decisions based on the holistic data (e.g., take into account operational costs as well as rental or capital costs);

- Specialized tools to support decision-making (e.g., space-demand-scenario planning linked to future financial maintenance liabilities); and

- Ability to integrate external data, such as financial transactions or employee data linked to assigned seating from other enterprise systems.

Conclusion

A wide range of technology tools for managing corporate real estate portfolios is available. No one approach or software solution is best in all circumstances. Companies must select the approach that best meets their needs.

In particular, the capabilities of integrated workplace management systems have increased dramatically in recent years. These systems represent today's state of the art in corporate real estate technology platforms. Still, as part of the CoreNet Global Corporate Real Estate 2020 study, participant Peter Miscovich of Jones Lang LaSalle said big changes are coming within corporate real estate technology.

"I think some of the 'Big Data' and advanced analytics technologies that are coming from the IT world will be very powerful, and these IT analytical tools may supersede many of the current integrated workplace management systems (IWMS) that are being offered today," he stated.[7]

References

1. Wales, P. (2015). *Driving the strategic decision: Why more companies are moving to IWMS.* Article from eBusiness Strategies. Retrieved from http://www.realcomm.com/advisory/674/1/driving-the-strategic-decision-why-more-companies-are-moving-to-iwms

2. Bouri, G. (2007, May/June). Leveraging Technology to Increase Corporate Real Estate's Value Proposition to the Enterprise. *The Leader.* Retrieved from https://resources.corenetglobal.org/knowledgecenteronline/SearchByTopicAndResource.aspx?ID=4375

3. Wales, P. (2012). Top 10 barriers to an IWMS implementation. Retrieved from http://www.iwmsnews.com/2012/11/top-10-barriers-to-an-iwms-implementation/

4. McDonald, J. (2015). 5 Brutally Honest Reasons You Aren't Implementing an IWMS. Retrieved from http://www.iofficecorp.com/blog/5-brutally-honest-reasons-you-arent-implementing-an-iwms

5. Schafer, R. (2013). *Magic quadrant for integrated workplace management systems.* Report from Gartner, Inc. Retrieved from http://static1.squarespace.com/static/53503de4e4b09b70f38f96a9/t/537e1185e4b073a7c434ded5/1400770949609/iwms

6. United Nations Environment Programme Sustainable Buildings and Climate Initiative. Retrieved from www.unep.org/sbci/AboutSBCI/Background.asp

7. CoreNet Global. (2012). *Corporate real estate 2020 final report: Technology tools.* Retrieved from https://resources.corenetglobal.org/knowledgecenteronline/SearchByTopicAndResource.aspx?ID=4273

Chapter 11

Project Management

Summary

The Project Management Institute, one of dozens of similar organizations worldwide, defines project management in general as "the application of knowledge, skills and techniques to execute projects effectively and efficiently."[1] It goes on to say that project management responsibilities are strategic in nature, allowing organizations to link project results with business goals.

In corporate real estate, project management is most often associated with construction activities related to the life cycle of real estate ownership or control. This includes the original development, required building or office renovations, restack—or reorganization of the workplace—and eventual exit and decommissioning. (A restack involves reorganizing the workplace—particularly in a multilevel building—to minimize redundant space while creating a more efficient and collaborative setting.)[2] In the loosest terms, a project manager is tasked with delivering a completed work product on time, within budget, and with specific resources.

Depending on the venture, the project manager works for the real estate owner or an outside consultancy. The owner could be a real estate developer or landlord, but it could also be a corporate occupier in an owner-occupied building.

Whether the project manager works for the owner or for an outside consultancy, he or she will regard the employer as his or her customer. The employer will have a clearly defined role to play in most forms of contracts, whether for consultant appointments or in building contracts. This clear definition of the employer / client role is essential when developing the project brief, regardless of the structure.

Additionally, corporate occupiers of leased space in multi-tenant office buildings often hire project managers to oversee real estate- and workplace-related projects, such as tenant improvements.

A project manager's loyalties can be split between a direct employer and the property or project owner. In this scenario, it is very important that the project owner understand how the project manager's employment is structured. The project owner must ensure that no conflicts of interest exist and that the project manager is working in the best interest of the proposal.

The term "project management" is often confused—or used interchangeably—with "*construction* project management" or, simply and erroneously, "construction management." Construction management, however, refers to a consultant who works similarly to a general contractor to deliver an overall construction project. It is more accurate to say the project manager manages construction work, which can include preliminary planning activities that define the scope of the project, preconstruction site selection, and all the due diligence associated with preparing for the project to come. It can also include budgeting and scheduling and post-construction work.

Following site selection and preparation, the project manager works to ensure the project is completed according to plan. He or she works extensively with architects and general contractors or construction managers to oversee or directly manage all design, procurement, construction, and financial aspects of the project. This closely follows the Project Management Institute's description of the process, which is initiating, planning, executing, monitoring, controlling, and closing.

What Is a Project?

Project management is also often confused with *program management*. The distinction here is that a project has very clear start and end dates and is assigned resources temporarily. A *program* manager, on the other hand, is one who oversees an ongoing program of work in any given area, which might include *project* activity. Project management is often outsourced because of its temporary nature. To further explain the distinction, a program manager might oversee a number of individual projects that run concurrently; each would have its own project manager who reports to the program manager. This is a very common approach with large organizations that have multiple projects in multiple locations.

Real estate project development can imply the limited lifespan of a particular development and is often used to distinguish a temporary, tactical project from the broader term "real estate development," which describes an entire business sector.

Perhaps the word *project* causes confusion regarding the difference between a project manager and a construction manager. Every construction management activity is a project, but not every project management activity involves construction. For example, a project manager might oversee the enterprise-wide installation of new computer equipment or the retrofitting of all of the company's properties with energy-saving LED lighting. In these cases, the required skill set is that of a well-organized facilitator for every aspect of the operation in order for the process to reach a final, successful outcome.

Another example of a project might be a lease termination and subsequent transition. The occupier would need a project manager to handle the initial analysis, exit strategy, lease acquisition, office design, procurement, and delivery, including all aspects of the relocation. In large corporations, these functions might be further divided, but the project manager is a vital part of the assigned team.

Project Management As a Career Path

Project management has taken on a formal meaning as a career option only in recent years. This formality includes a more rigid construct for job qualifications and the value a project manager can bring to an organization, such as project savings, market knowledge, or seamless coordination of all the participants. Like a strong facility manager, a strong project manager can minimize costs and add value to any project. Increasingly, the emphasis is on the "value add" and ensuring that daily business is not disrupted for the underlying organization.

Today, certifications in project management can be earned in a variety of fields following concentrated study. In many cases, college-based project management certifications related to the real estate industry are specifically geared to *construction* project management. These certifications are valuable to the professional who wants to gain pre- or post-construction experience and to work on the client side (e.g., for the corporate occupier).

Qualifying As a Real Estate Project Manager

A successful real estate project manager needs a variety of skills. In general terms, the Project Management Institute recognizes 10 distinct areas of knowledge and project attributes when awarding the field's most notable certification, the Project Management Professional (PMP)® certification. These include:

- Integration
- Scope
- Time
- Cost
- Quality
- Procurement
- Human resources
- Communications
- Risk management
- Stakeholder management

This base of knowledge is directly related to project management in real estate. For example, stakeholder management in real estate might involve addressing the owner's interest in a tighter schedule, the local municipality's desire for maximized tax revenue, neighboring companies' request for certain landscape design elements, or an environmental group's demand to abandon building plans. Resolving these multiple issues appropriately (and diplomatically) is a major challenge for the project management professional.[3]

Likewise, communication skills for the real estate development project manager will involve tactful and productive interpersonal relations with other owner representatives as well as a host of other on-site professionals. In addition to the general contractor, a project manager will interact with multiple engineers, architects, designers, various real estate professionals, tax and financial specialists, and more.

As an owner representative, the real estate project manager embraces corporate values and executes projects accordingly. That might include making diligent efforts to mitigate the environmental impact of a proposal. The U.S. Green Building Council, a leading advocate of environmentally sensitive building, certifies real estate professionals with LEED credentials.

Depending on the type of development pursued, an owner might specify other qualifications from the project management candidate, particularly for jobs involving specialized real estate. In a 2014 project management job posting by Apple, the high-tech firm stated the need for a candidate to have a mechanical engineering degree in addition to commercial or industrial construction experience for overseeing development projects based out of its corporate office in Santa Clara Valley, California.[4] Such niche employment opportunities can draw top candidates to top salaries.

A Closer Look at Project Management

Project management proceeds through a clearly defined set of phases, according to the Project Management Institute:

- Initiating
- Planning
- Executing
- Monitoring and controlling
- Closing

In the corporate real estate profession, the life cycle of a project is typically defined in a more streamlined fashion:

- Planning
- Designing
- Construction
- Close-out

Below, each phase, as described by the Project Management Institute, and how it relates to corporate real estate will be examined.

Initiating

The standard business tool for initiating a project is a charter or brief. This device clearly defines the basic but essential elements of a project: its scope, goal or purpose, the assigned project manager, and the required organizational resources. It also serves as the formal document to authorize and fund the project.[5] In real estate, contracts are typically used when a project is outsourced. Internally, a job description should clearly indicate the need for these critical steps.

Also critical is the need to determine what defines a project's success and how that success will be measured. Potential yardsticks include whether the project is delivered "on time and on budget" or high marks on a follow-up tenant satisfaction survey.

Planning

Failures of real estate projects have broad implications. They can negatively affect a company's brand and reputation and have dire consequences for the company's ability to meet overall business objectives or—in the worst cases—remain viable.[6] Project planning, then, should employ a specific, time-tested series of guidelines in order to minimize risk factors that can affect the project's long-term success.

In traditional, general business, project-management terms, overall planning involves preparing for each project attribute described in the Project Management Professional certification, which was discussed above. For example, there is a planning stage for integrating multiple disciplines into the current project, and frameworks are created outlining the project's scope, timeframe, cost, quality measurements, and procurement processes. Necessary human resources and potential risks are identified in the overall planning stage, and a communications matrix is created to identify all project stakeholders so that each can be provided necessary information in the most appropriate, way.[5]

However, things can go wrong even with the best plans, and being too inflexible in the design or execution phases of the process can set projects up for failure. Flexibility must be built into the project to ensure better outcomes, and proper communication must facilitate a coordinated effort to correct any problems within reasonable timeframes and cost structures.

Communication is enhanced by a common language that ensures all parties possess a common working knowledge of the project. Ensuring that all are "on the same page" regarding what can seem to be the simplest things, such as industry terminology or overall processes within each project, helps to mitigate risk and provide clarity.

A common language can also help the property and / or project owner and the project management establish business requirements and manage expectations. The tongue-in-cheek adage, "fast, good, and cheap: pick any two," actually provides a fairly accurate description of the project management triangle. It illustrates in simple terms the idea that a project's speed, quality, and cost will never align optimally—one will always suffer at the expense of the other two. Several variations of the concept exist; scope is often the third side of the triangle along with time and cost and quality in the center as the common project denominator. The idea, however, is the same, and its message is clear. A project manager must be able to communicate how a change in expectations for one aspect of the project—such as cost—will affect other aspects of the project. Every decision has consequences.

Executing

Executing a real estate project is no small feat, and the formal project management structure can be applied to projects of varying scope. All processes for carrying out the development plan and meeting project objectives are implemented in the executing phase, which is applied to six knowledge areas or project attributes: integration, quality, human resources, communications, procurement, and stakeholders.[5] The executing phase involves directing and managing the project; identifying, training, and managing the project team; distributing information; soliciting and acquiring project materials; managing expectations of all stakeholders; and assuring project quality during all phases of development.[3]

For distributing information about real estate development projects, KPMG's Relle and Gilge recommend a monthly project report to communicate "progress, issues, concerns, financial status, earned value and other key information about the project."[7]

In the corporate real estate environment, the need for strong communication skills cannot be overstated. Considering the permanency of the work, the amount of money involved, and the number and diversity of stakeholders, a successful project manager must be able to communicate effectively at every level, with every stakeholder, while managing individual day-to-day activities. Because communication is so critical to the success of a project, often team members who were involved in the initiating and planning stages remain involved for the sake of effective communication, consistency, and project accountability.

Monitoring and Controlling

To keep projects from straying off target, ongoing monitoring of the processes and controls should be performed. In pure project management terms, monitoring and controlling works much like planning. Monitors and controls are established for each of the 10 knowledge areas of the project management process—from integration to communication to risk management—to ensure the goals established during the planning phase are attainable. If not, controls identified in the planning phase are implemented. This structure assures that any changes in the project's execution can then trigger the appropriate changes to other aspects of the process and prevent the need for further corrections.[3]

An additional step can be establishing preliminary expectations on the part of the project owner. For at least one Middle East development project, PricewaterhouseCoopers' capital project services followed a set of monitoring and control guidelines that, in the company's words, fulfilled "a hierarchy of needs" of internal stakeholders. The guidelines ensured that:

- Capital was being deployed effectively;

- Risks were being managed;

- The ROI was being maximized;

- The project viability was regularly being tested;

- The benefits were aligned with end-user needs;

- Decisions were made at the appropriate levels; and

- Reporting was accurate and timely.[6]

Closing

When a development or renovation project is completed, project management constructs dictate that the project end formally, with appropriate notifications given to all those brought into the project in the integration and procurement phases. All project activities, such as contracts and open items, are resolved and finalized, and information collected during the project is archived. Lessons learned during the project also are recorded and maintained for future reference.[5]

Conclusion

Relatively speaking, project management is a newly *defined* field although the practice of project management is not. It is constantly evolving to meet ever-changing client requirements. Project management within a corporate real estate environment should not be seen simply as the management of construction work, but as part of the planning and implementation of activities by numerous parties. Successful project management should deliver a product that meets the employer's intentions.

There is no shortage of project management service providers as services are offered by commercial real estate firms, independent third parties, architects, and design and consulting firms globally. Because of its temporary nature, project management is among the disciplines most readily outsourced by building owners and owner-occupiers.

Organizations that possess internal real estate project management capabilities should determine methods for keeping projects delivered on time and on budget. A real estate project can lay a solid foundation for successful execution of a venture by employing the steps established for traditional, general business, project management.

References

1. Project Management Institute. (n.d.). *What is project management?* Retrieved from http://www.pmi.org/About-Us/About-Us-What-is-Project-Management.aspx

2. Lander, L. F. (2012, Summer). In focus: Re-stack brings efficiency, collaboration to the workplace. *Area Development.* Retrieved from http://www.areadevelopment.com/siteSelection/Summer2012/restacking-workspace-Lander-PDR-Corporation-2522221.shtml

3. Duncan, W. (1996). *A guide to the project management body of knowledge.* Retrieved from http://www.itq.ch/pdf/pmbok1.pdf

4. Apple, Inc. (2014). Project manager, real estate and development. Retrieved from https://jobs.apple.com/us/search?#mixes&fMix=current&apply=0&t=1&sb=req_open_dt&so=1&j=FACLT&lo=0*USA&pN=0&openJobId=36910772

5. Pulverenti, R., & Scherzi, D. (2013). *PMBOK 5: Update & maintaining your PMP.* Syracuse, NY: PMI Syracuse.

6. Broadhead, N., Wilhelmij, P., & Roe, J. (2010). Establishing a basis for effective project control. *PricewaterhouseCoopers LLP Capital Project Services.* Retrieved from http://www.pwc.com/en_M1/m1/services/deals/CPS-effective-project-control.pdf

7. Relle, B., & Gilge, C. (2013). *KPMG/building, construction & real estate: How to successfully manage your mega-project.* Retrieved from https://www.kpmg.com/US/en/IssuesAndInsights/ArticlesPublications/Documents/manage-mega-project-2.pdf

8. Eli Lilly & Co. (2013, March). *Innovating & realizing a project delivery model in Asia.* Presentation at CoreNet Global Summit 2013, Shanghai. Retrieved from: https://resources.corenetglobal.org/knowledgecenteronline/SearchByTopicAndResource.aspx?ID=5385

Chapter 12

Sustainability

Summary

In 1983, the United Nations Brundtland Commission was formed, and charged with uniting countries around the world to pursue sustainable development together. In its 1987 report, "*Our Common Future*," the group defined sustainability as: "development which meets the needs of current generations without compromising the ability of future generations to meet their own needs."[1]

A vast departure from the practices of manufacturing, building, and operating regardless of environmental consequences, what began as a small advocacy initiative has snowballed into a major global movement. Driven by concerns over climate change and limited natural resources, sustainability has morphed from a novelty into a baseline requirement in today's real estate industry.

In the context of real estate, the U.S. Environmental Protection Agency defines "green building" as the practice of creating structures and utilizing processes that are environmentally responsible and resource-efficient throughout the building's full life-cycle. This includes factors such as where and how the building is located, design, construction, operation, maintenance, renovation, deconstruction, and disposal.

The term *corporate social responsibility* (CSR) has been adopted by many in and out of the corporate world as a way to encourage organizations to accept greater responsibility for their sizable environmental footprints. In addition, sustainability reporting has been embraced by many organizations, meaning they have shifted operations so that their decisions are not based solely on financial considerations, but also take into account environmental, social, and ethical standards as well.

While progress has been made, work still remains. According to a 2011 survey, *Reducing Waste and Increasing Value through Corporate Energy Management,* conducted by CoreNet Global and the Johnson Controls Institute for Building Efficiency, corporate energy management is still in nascent form. "While most organizations have adopted at least one approach for managing energy consumption, very few have instilled a culture of efficient energy use throughout the enterprise," according to the report.[2]

Strategy for Sustainable Development

The good news is that sustainability is a critical business issue for 70% of respondents participating in a 2009 CoreNet Global/Jones Lang LaSalle global survey, and 89% consider sustainability criteria in their location decisions.[3] Meanwhile, 89% evaluate the possibility of green building certification, and 90% consider energy labels in administering their portfolio.

In order to build a business case, it will be necessary to develop a real-estate focused sustainability platform. In addition, it will then be important to establish ownership and executive sponsorship of the program, in addition to getting employees on board. This effort must include communicating the vision, fostering participation, building culture, and encouraging innovation. Both design and operational standards should then be aligned with organizational sustainability goals, and the company's supply chain should be leveraged to facilitate objectives and multiply these positive impacts.

Materiality Analysis

In order to get buy-in from the organization's stakeholders, corporate real estate executives should consider conducting a materiality analysis to determine which issues are most important to stakeholders, who are "ranked" based upon how they influence or are influenced by the company and the extent of responsibility the organization has to them. This analysis then compares how important each issue is to the stakeholders versus the level of importance the company places on each issue. For example, a priority matrix can help evaluate the issues from the points of view of stakeholders, users, occupants, company management, and others.

To assist them in this process, companies can use resources such as AcountAbility's AA1000 (available at http://www.accountability.org), an internationally recognized stakeholder engagement standard, and a similar resource offered by the Global Reporting Initiative (https://www.globalreporting.org), which is an internationally accepted, voluntary, sustainable framework used by many organizations.

Three Basic Tenets

A joint study by CoreNet Global and the Rocky Mountain Institute in 2007 describes a framework companies can follow to improve energy utilization when stakeholders are on board. According to the study, *The Energy Challenge: A New Agenda for Corporate Real Estate,* organizations should:

- Articulate a clear and compelling vision of a more energy-efficient future supported by specific objectives transparent to all stakeholders—including local communities, employees, shareholders, and suppliers.

- Work with energy suppliers and others in the corporate real estate supply chain; use the request for proposal process as a tool to reduce energy utilization in owned or leased facilities; and set target levels for performance based on historical data.

- Continuously measure energy consumption and performance on a systematic, real-time basis to track success and identify areas that can be corrected or improved. These steps are often documented as low-cost solutions.[4]

Sustainable Strategies

In addition, CoreNet Global and Johnson Control's Institute for Building Efficiency offered the following list of sustainable development strategies for organizations in their 2011 study:[2]

- Adopt a formal standard, such as ANSI, ISO, or Energy Star, for energy management.

- Develop a dedicated, formal policy. Similar to employee safety or product quality policies, an energy management policy could include ideas about how to propose and evaluate projects or requirements for tracking energy performance.

- Publicly communicate a quantitative goal, such as a target for overall energy use reduction, in order to increase accountability. This can be a month-to-month energy budget.

- Develop a detailed, organization-wide, action plan with protocols and best practices in order to bridge the gap between goals and results.

- Encourage C-level responsibility. Chances of success are increased if senior management is on board.

- Establish and empower dedicated teams for managing energy.

- Train employees to adopt good habits, such as turning off lights and shutting down computer monitors.

- Establish incentives for energy efficiency results, such as bonuses to facility operations staff.

- Establish ways to gather and monitor data. By establishing organizational practices such as analysis techniques, and measurement and verification requirements, an organization can effectively utilize valuable energy consumption data and chart a clear course to energy improvement.

- Instill a periodic review. Initiatives and policies should be revisited, audited, reviewed, reevaluated, and refined.

Variety of Goals

Ultimately, an organization should have environmental, economic, and social goals. For example, an environmental agenda could include enhancing and protecting biodiversity and ecosystems, improving air and water quality, reducing waste streams, and conserving and restoring natural resources.

On the economic side, companies should be taking steps to reduce operating costs; create, expand, and shape markets for sustainable and energy-efficient products and services; improve occupant productivity, health, and well-being; and optimize life-cycle economic performance.

Social goals can include enhancing occupant comfort and health, heightening aesthetic qualities, minimizing strain on the local infrastructure, and improving overall quality of life.

Sustainability Commitment Spectrum

Ilse van de Voort, a consultant with the Netherlands-based engineering and project management firm, Royal Haskoning DHV, can help organizations understand where they fit on the spectrum of sustainability commitment levels. In a 2014 CoreNet Global presentation, she offered the following measurements:[5]

Inactive. "Sustainability is a government task that limits me." Focus on cost efficiency and optimization.

Reactive. "We do it because we have to." Company sets targets and commits to limited reporting.

Active. "Sustainability is a commercial opportunity." The supply chain is engaged, and full reporting becomes the standard.

Proactive. "We are a change agent in sustainability." All stakeholders are involved, and the company proactively initiates programs.

At the same time, van de Voort cautions against abandoning goals in the face of opposition. "When euphoria about formulated sky-high ambitions start to fade, and implementation appears to mismatch budgets, reverting to the business as usual appears to be the logical step."[5]

In order to prevent this move, van de Voort stresses the importance of setting sustainability goals that suit the identity of the organization. In this way, beliefs are established and the company can start taking the actions that match its economic reality.

To assist organizations with their sustainable development goals, a number of green certification programs and other tools are available. In addition to providing a systematic approach to chart sustainability, some of these programs are a great way for an organization to publicize its commitment to sustainability.

Corporate Social Responsibility Reports

For starters, a corporate social responsibility report is an internationally recognized way for an organization to publicly communicate its economic, governance, environmental, and social performance. As described in the white paper, *Sustainability Reporting Guideline Mapping & Gap Analyses*, published by the International Finance Corporation, the following six factors are needed for a report on corporate social responsibility.[6]

Materiality and completeness. The report should cover the company's reporting period and all topics and indicators that reflect the company's economical, environmental, and social impacts.

Stakeholder engagement. Stakeholders, expectations, interests, and inter-relationships should all be identified and discussed.

Fair balance. Both positive and negative outcomes of corporate sustainability performance should be reflected accurately.

Comparability. Including globally accepted indicators and data, consistent across years, will allow those within and outside the organization to analyze its progress over time.

Timeliness. Reporting should take place on a regular basis and be made available in a timely fashion to stakeholders so that they can make informed decisions.

Reliability. The process of gathering information should be recorded and analyzed for quality and traceability, and the data should be subject to external examination.

Social Responsibility Motivation

Motivation for sustainability reporting varies among organizations, ranging from marketplace pressure, brand value, risk management, and other variables. Whatever the motivation, 81% of all major companies have corporate social responsibility information published on their websites, according to a 2010 Craib Design & Communication/Pricewaterhouse Coopers report.[7]

Furthermore, the report states that corporate social responsibility programs are now "addressing issues that once took a back seat to financial results—if they had a seat at all—and have become critical to a company's credibility, transparency and endurance."[7]

Even more compelling, when corporate social responsibility becomes an integral part of business planning, companies perform better, according to a 2011 article in *The Leader*, "Building the Bridge: Positioning Corporate Real Estate for the New Corporate Metrics," by Perkins+Will workplace strategy consultants Janice Barnes and Carolyn Roose and Keith Perske, a mobility practice leader with eBusiness Strategies.[8] Drawing this conclusion based upon recent studies by Bloomberg and Jantzi-Sustainalytics, the *Leader* authors go on to suggest this may have a direct impact on the value of a company's stock:

> With an immediate strategic position to consider, organizations are shifting their attention to CSR and its value proposition. It's more than reporting; corporate leaders now seek alignment throughout their companies to ensure that reporting is not de-facto, but instead focused on performance targets that contribute to industry evaluation.[8]

Indicators, Agendas, and Organizations

In order to create corporate social responsibility reports, organizations can either develop their own indicators or look to formats created by organizations such as Ceres, a nonprofit group that promotes sustainable leadership, or the well-established Global Reporting Initiative.

The Global Reporting Initiative is a network-based organization with more than 600 core supporters from more than 60 countries representing the business world, academia, and public agencies. As of late 2014, close to 21,000 sustainability reports were registered in its database.

In addition, the CoreNet Global Sustainable Strategies MCR seminar goes beyond corporate social responsibility reporting to set forth a number of programs available to help organizations pursue and achieve sustainable agendas.

For example, the International Organization for Standardization's ISO 14000 family of standards is all about environmental management.[9] Designed for organizations interested in identifying, controlling, and improving their environmental performance, ISO 14000 covers topics such as life-cycle analysis, communication, and auditing.

Another important initiative is the Carbon Disclosure Project, which has collected primary information on climate change, water, and forest-risk activities from more than 5,000 companies worldwide. Ranked as the most credible sustainability survey by 800 global sustainability professionals, investors turn to Carbon Disclosure Project data when analyzing environmental risk exposure.[10]

The Dow Jones Sustainability Index is another indicator.[11] As the first global sustainability benchmark, this index tracks the stock performance of major global companies based on economic, environmental, and social criteria.

A rigorous program, Cradle to Cradle Certification, rewards organizations and products that achieve particular environmental and social responsibility goals. Directed by the Cradle to Cradle Products Innovation Institute, the label is awarded when companies successfully transform their manufacturing and operating processes to meet the following five criteria: 100% renewable energy use, clean water output, a positive impact on their community, material reutilization via recycling / composting, and having a positive human and environmental impact. A company can also boost its commitment to sustainability by specifying such products must be used when it is constructing or retrofitting a space.

Green Building Certification Programs

A wide range of green building certification programs are available to corporate real estate professionals. Widely used in the United States, as well as in other countries, is the U.S. Green Building Council's well-established LEED (Leadership in Energy and Environmental Design) building certification system. Evolving to keep up with sustainability building trends, LEED sets a consistent standard for owners and tenants with regional portfolios.

Overseen by the U.S. Environmental Protection Agency, the Energy Star program scores buildings from 1 to 100, based upon strict energy performance standards. According to 2012 EPA statistics, more than 20,000 buildings and plants are Energy Star certified, and more than 300,000 commercial buildings are actively measuring and tracking their energy use. The goal for each building is to decrease energy use and increase their energy start score each year.

Established in the United Kingdom in 1990, BREEAM (Building Research Establishment's Environmental Assessment Method) is now widely used across Europe and in other countries to certify green buildings. Approximately 425,000 buildings around the world have certified BREEAM assessment ratings.

LEED, Energy Star and BREEAM are just three examples of green building certification programs. Regardless of the program used, being able to prove a facility is energy-conscious can improve marketability and rental rates. Prospective tenants often desire disclosure of energy, water, and resource use metrics, per square foot, for a facility.

The Economics of Sustainability

While few will dispute that sustainable development is ethical and environmentally responsible, it still has to make financial sense. Thus, organizations must build a business case for sustainability. Fortunately, energy-efficient retrofits have become widely recognized as a strategy to reduce costs and boost corporate image, according to the above-referenced CoreNet Global/Johnson Controls white paper.[2] In fact, the cost savings and operational benefits provided by improved energy efficiency has risen to best-practice prominence, comparable to strategies like "lean manufacturing" and Six Sigma, the report authors say.

Recent studies show a direct correlation between an active energy management program and stock market performance. In particular, the EPA estimates that every dollar invested in energy efficiency boosts asset value by $3 USD. This being the case, energy efficiency can be viewed as a low-risk, high-return investment.

Barriers to Sustainability

However, it's easier to talk about sustainability programs than to create and maintain them. Within a typical real estate organization, it's not uncommon for different entities to find themselves competing for limited investment capital for building improvement projects. For example, the portfolio manager may want to keep the real estate's investment needs to a minimum, while a property manager would like to increase operational efficiencies, thereby requiring significant capital improvements.

"Building a financial model whereby real estate managers can evaluate competing investment alternatives will assist the manager in making more informed decisions," advises Kristian Peterson, LEED green associate and director of consulting at Sustainability Roundtable. She and Ross Gammill, director of commercial due diligence at Allonhill, a mortgage due diligence and credit risk management services company, wrote an IFMA Foundation-sponsored white paper, *The Economics of Sustainability in Commercial Real Estate.*[12]

"The objective of using a financial model is to apply return metrics that various real estate managers use to analyze an investment, and to then compare the order of magnitude of the various returns," they explain.

Expectations for Sustainability Features

Although building owners and landlords may consider the barriers to efficiency investments, they must account for the fact that more and more tenants, particularly high-profile corporations, are likely to look for sustainability features in leased buildings. Corporate responsibility reports are an increasingly important aspect of a company's annual report, which is carefully studied by industry analysts and shareholders. Ultimately, these stakeholders want to see a visible commitment to sustainable business practices.

Role of Real Estate Professionals

Corporate real estate leaders should consider taking on more of a leadership role in order to inspire sustainability measures within their organizations. In fact, the CoreNet Global *Corporate Real Estate 2020 Sustainability Report* states that—in addition to aligning real estate—real estate managers must influence business leadership, procurement, public relations, marketing, human resources, information technology, research and development, operations and logistics, health and safety, legal and risk management in order to make sustainability a more inherent part of the company culture.[13]

"Real estate must be able to weave 'environmentally friendly' strategies into a larger story that benefits the organization," advises the report. "Corporate real estate leaders who expand their business case are more likely to build traction and have their ideas adopted."[13]

References

1. United Nations. (1987). *Report of the World Commission on Environment and Development: Our common future.* Retrieved from http://www.un-documents.net/our-common-future.pdf

2. CoreNet Global & Johnson Controls Institute for Building Efficiency. (2011). *Reducing waste and increasing value through corporate energy management.* Retrieved from https://resources.corenetglobal.org/knowledgecenteronline/SearchByTopicAndResource.aspx?ID=6230

3. CoreNet Global & Jones Lang LaSalle. (2009). *Perspectives on sustainability.* Retrieved from https://resources.corenetglobal.org/knowledgecenteronline/SearchByTopicAndResource.aspx?ID=2418

4. CoreNet Global & Rocky Mountain Institute. (2007). *The energy challenge: A new agenda for corporate real estate.* Available from https://resources.corenetglobal.org/knowledgecenteronline/SearchByTopicAndResource.aspx?ID=952

5. Van de Voort, I. (2014, March). "Setting your ambitions right, it delivers!" Presentation at CoreNet Global Singapore Summit. Retrieved from https://resources.corenetglobal.org/knowledgecenteronline/SearchByTopicAndResource.aspx?ID=2187

6. International Finance Corporation. (2011). *Sustainability reporting guideline mapping & gap analyses.* Retrieved from http://www.ifc.org/wps/wcm/connect/19231a80488658 5bb596f76a6515bb18/SSE_IFCReport+English.pdf?MOD=AJPERES&CACHEID= 19231a804886585bb596f76a6515bb18

7. Craib & Pricewaterhouse Coopers. (2010). *CSR trends 2010.* Retrieved from https://www.pwc.com/ca/en/sustainability/publications/csr-trends-2010-09.pdf

8. Barnes, J., Roose, C., & Perske, K. (2011, September/October). Building the bridge: Positioning corporate real estate for the new corporate metrics. *The Leader.* Retrieved from https://resources.corenetglobal.org/knowledgecenteronline/SearchByTopicAndResource.aspx?ID=5222?ID=1542

9. International Organization for Standardization. (2010). *Environmental management: The ISO 14000 family of international standards.* Retrieved from http://www.iso.org/iso/home/store/publication_item.htm?pid=PUB100238

10. Carbon Disclosure Project. (n.d.). Retrieved from https://www.cdp.net/en-US/Pages/HomePage.aspx

11. RobecoSam & Dow Jones. (n.d.). *Dow Jones sustainability indices.* Retrieved from http://www.sustainability-indices.com/about-us/dow-jones-sustainability-indices.jsp

12. Peterson, K., & Gammill, R. (2010). *The economics of sustainability in commercial real estate.* IMFA Foundation. Retrieved from https://resources.corenetglobal.org/knowledgecenteronline/SearchByTopicAndResource.aspx?ID=5279

13. CoreNet Global. (2012). *Corporate real estate 2020 sustainability report.* Retrieved from https://resources.corenetglobal.org/knowledgecenteronline/SearchByTopicAndResource.aspx?ID=4892

Chapter 13

Workplace Strategy, Mobility and Productivity

Summary

Employees in today's progressive workplace often encounter a vastly different scene than their counterparts experienced a few years ago. Instead of clocking in and then settling into a cubicle while the boss looks on from the corner office, workers today are arriving to find workplaces that are arranged in a variety of ways to meet a variety of needs.

The workplace environment is evolving to address a whirlwind of variables, including a need to encourage collaborative working arrangements and a desire to address sustainability issues. In addition, many organizations include multiple generations who have very different viewpoints on working styles. These factors have combined to create a highly adaptable, and sometimes complicated, workplace environment.

For starters, many employees are no longer required to be tethered to their office workstation. On the contrary, they are provided with the freedom and connectivity to produce work in a variety of settings: inside the office, at home, on the go, or in second and third spaces—such as incubator spaces or the local coffee house.

Changing workforce demographics and employee expectations, continuing economic challenges, spreading globalization, and rapidly changing technology bring new realities and new ways of working. Organizations that are open to adopting a new workplace strategy are more likely to maintain a competitive advantage.

New Ways of Working

As a starting point, CoreNet Global defines the term "workplace strategy" as a process of aligning an organization's workplaces to support its strategic business goals, while optimizing real estate performance. This strategy is developed based upon a number of dimensions within the company—including its physical and virtual work environments, culture, behaviors, business processes, technologies, and other resources—with the ultimate goal of encouraging people to work in ways that support the organization's mission.

Traditional ways of working are now being replaced by emerging styles:

- Place as a series of activities to help produce innovation instead of a destination for work;

- Performance based on results instead of on time clocked;

- Mentoring, coaching and enabling instead of supervision;

- Mobile, virtual teams instead of co-locating team members; and

- Space allocation based on functional work practices instead of hierarchy.

Based upon today's working styles, yesterday's space occupancy floor plans and technological tools are largely inadequate. For example, consider the typical traditional conference room. Today, these rooms are largely underutilized as they are much too big for smaller meetings and fail to support multiple-person connectivity, virtual collaboration, or information display. However, an environment that provides different-sized rooms with a variety of furniture styles—from the traditional table and chairs to soft seating for more casual meetings—supports the types of collaboration that are being encouraged in the workplace today.

Technology Requirements

In addition, effective workplaces also require a dynamic booking system to support better utilization and up-to-date technological tools such as Wi-Fi, LCD screens, smart boards, and interactive conferencing. To begin addressing the technology component, today's workplaces absolutely must offer secure connectivity to company data through multiple devices, increased network bandwidth, better collaboration tools, wireless connectivity, ubiquitous security, and robust technology platforms for e-mail, instant messaging, shared files, calendar management, audio and video conferencing, and adequate data storage.

Work Style Profiles

In addition, companies should perform a thorough evaluation of work style profiles and preferences to determine how to best support their employees by first understanding how they work.

Profile descriptions such as a *team anchor, knowledge worker,* and *independent* give others a general sense of each individual's functional role. When employees are given the opportunity to choose, some will prefer to work at home; others will opt for internal mobility inside the office and/ or other company locations; and still others will choose external mobility, such as working from a second or third space.

Mobility

Making the case for alternative workplace strategy and mobility, Irina Mladenova and Michael Gresty describe the benefits by department in Figure 13.1.[1]

RE	HR	IT
• Optimized RE; increased agility • Reduced costs • Reduced GHG emissions • Enhanced brand and reputation	• Increased productivity • Increased collaboration, innovation • Enhanced well-being • Improve employee attraction and retention • AWS regulations	• Enhanced network security • Reduced IT infrastructure and operating expense • Showcase technology

Figure 13.1. Benefits of Alternative Workplace Strategy, Mobility

The research and consulting firm Global Workplace Analytics reports that one in five Americans works from home—at least part-time—and that number is expected to increase dramatically.[2]

Looking toward the future, one of the bold statements included in the CoreNet Global *Corporate Real Estate 2020 Report* predicts that workplace mobility will evolve to encompass the concept of "presence."[3] That is, companies will expand the range of places where their employees are "present" and actively accomplishing the various requirements of their work.

Ultimately, experts emphasize the importance of letting the worker determine the "how, when and where," as long as agreed-to expectations and results are met. In other words, the notion of work should be what you do, not where you do it.

The Evolving Office

While a number of workers will choose to work at home or another locale, the office still plays a central role in the workplace experience. In a 2012 *Corporate Real Estate 2020* research one-on-one interview, Franklin Becker, then a professor in the department of design and environmental analysis at Cornell University, stated that today's younger workers still want office time so they can feel part of something, to be around highly productive people, and to take advantage of learning opportunities that informally arise in the workplace.[3] There is no form of virtual connectivity that can replace a face–to-face interaction.

In another 2012 interview for Corporate Real Estate 2020, Mark Gorman, MCR, SLCR, vice president, corporate real estate and facilities, Ciena, explains that his company does have a telework program where employees can sign up for as many as two days per week.[3] However, Ciena highly values the opportunity for face-to-face contact and collaboration.

Space Options

Within the office environment, organizations can provide a variety of spaces to create optimal working conditions based upon worker preferences. Often referred to as *focus spaces*, individual or focus-area options include a variety of small open spaces. These spaces may be referred to as an enclave, cockpit, bullpen, touchdown, harvest table, or hive.

An enclave provides a small private space for one-on-one conversations, private telephone calls, and a place for heads-down work. A cockpit is a small, reservable, single-person space intended to provide privacy. A bullpen setting is an open team space where collaboration is key to the job. A touchdown is a small desk or table, which can be at counter or desk height, to provide a worker with a place to work for an hour or two between meetings. A harvest table is as it sounds, a common table where a group can work either together or individually, like in a library. Finally, the hive is often set up as 120-degree workstations for both heads-down and team work.

Group or collaborative spaces, both formal and informal, can be set up as an enclave, a scrum room to support a streamlined project management process, or a flexible conference room or project space. Common areas may encompass a quiet zone, open lounge, and break area or café.

"The future office needs a much greater diversity of settings—all carefully established through a robust process of understanding work practices and behaviors," recommends CBRE in a 2014 workplace strategy report titled *Why One Size Does Not Fit All.*[4]

Space Allocation

Trying out scenarios with different variables can help organizations determine the most effective options for their workers. This will help the company's real estate and design professionals understand the gains and losses associated with modifying different allocation variables. Ultimately, the organization can then determine the ratio of space allocation for open workstations, private offices, and support space.

Research by Gensler, as reported in the 2013 Workplace Index Survey, notes that only one in four U.S. workers are considered top performers.[5] Providing a workplace that delivers focus, balance, and choice to employees may enable them to perform at a higher level than organizations that do not adapt the environment around changing needs and preferences.

Demographics and Change

As corporate real estate professionals wade through the evolving variables shaping today's work culture, they need to keep in mind the needs and preferences of the upcoming millennial generation—individuals born between 1980 and 2002—who are now entering the workforce in increasing numbers. By 2030, the "iGen" or "Digital Natives," those born after 2002, will also begin to factor into the workplace.

Baby Boomers—defined as people born between 1946 and 1964—currently make up approximately 31% of the U.S. workforce, but their numbers are steadily declining as more and more of them reach retirement age. According to Gallup, Generation X, those with birthdays between 1965 and 1982, make up 32% of the workforce.[6]

Meanwhile, the millennials—also called generation Y—are the fastest growing workforce demographic. In 2010, the U.S. Bureau of Labor Statistics reported that millennials made up 37% of the total workplace. By 2020, they are projected to account for 51%. And by 2030, that number will jump to 75%.[7]

Generational Attitudes

Taking a tongue-in-cheek look at differing generational attitudes toward how to connect on various media, eBusiness Strategies, a CRE and workplace management consulting firm, describes boomers' opinions toward e-mail as "I can do that." Meanwhile, generation X calls email its "life blood," while millennials describe e-mails as "quaint."[8]

In a similar vein, anecdotal evidence would suggest the younger generation expects:

- More choice and control over where and when they work, including more say over balancing work and life;

- Access to files, data, and each other on demand, 24/7;

- Recognition for their contributions; and

- A chance to build communities within and outside their organization.

Many organizations are responding to the call and becoming more responsive to employees' personal needs. As explained in the CoreNet Global Corporate Real Estate 2020 workplace report, these responses are driven by a couple of factors.[3] For one, more and more corporations are viewing staff as their number one return on investment. Secondly, "newer generations of knowledge workers expect and demand some consideration for their personal lives. If they don't get it, they go elsewhere."

Without downplaying the millennials' impact on the workplace, it should be noted that what varies from generation to generation are the expectations of what the corporation will provide, *not* the individual behaviors within the workplace.

Corporate Empathy

For companies that prefer their employees to spend more time in the office, an effective strategy can be to supplement traditional workplace amenities with lifestyle enhancements such as on-site healthcare clinics, dry cleaners, gyms, and day care. "Provision of free and healthy food, recreational facilities, concierge support and playful work environments are often seen as signature elements," reports CBRE.[4]

As described in a *Corporate Real Estate 2020* visioning meeting report, "corporate empathy is fast becoming a key word in the 2020 business lexicon."[3]

Offering motivation for organizations to go that extra mile, studies directly link an enhanced work / life balance with higher job satisfaction and commitment and a stronger level of company engagement. For example, a 2011 Aon Hewitt survey found that companies with high levels of staff engagement—measured as 65% or greater—outperformed the total stock market index and shareholder returns by 22% above average firms. On the other hand, companies with weak staff engagement—45% or less— had a total shareholder return which was 28% lower than the average.

The Network

In *NetWork: the Future Workplace*, a white paper commissioned by Allsteel, architects Daniel P. Anderson and William Porter and environmental psychologist Judith Heerwagen identify a few overall trends driving workplace change:

- Power is shifting from more centralized organizational control to individuals, communities of practice, and social networks.

- Work and intellectual capabilities are now distributed and collective, rather than being vested in individuals.

- Making sense of large volumes of information and interactions requires analytical thinking and adaptive and social skills.

- The new "literacy" is based on the ability to build and use social networks.[9]

The authors go on to propose a newer network workplace theory which emphasizes work to be done and enabling workers to do that work most effectively rather than focusing on the traditional idea of the workplace as a place of work. To meet the new emphasis, only some workspaces should be purposefully designed whereas others will be allowed to dynamically evolve—with a "just in time" mentality—providing the furnishings, technologies, and equipment at the time when they are needed. This concept has been billed as an opportunity to link business processes to the workplace as opposed to employing "oversimplified, latest-trends-fit-all design to creating relevant, effective work settings."[9]

In a 2012 *Leader* article, "A Generation Ahead: Strategic Real Estate Planning Guide for Tomorrow's Work Force," authors Rob Larsen and Shawn Rush predict that the need for owned real estate will decline and be replaced by a leveraging of assets, from both within and outside an organization's portfolio, to meet specific needs.[10] As such, it is anticipated that corporations will be more likely to contract with third parties to deliver on-demand models for office space and technology.

In fact, a 2011 CoreNet Global survey revealed that, for the vast majority of companies, flexible working and the drive to reduce space started out as a real estate strategy but has now evolved into an overall business strategy.[11] What are organizations doing with this "extra" space? According to the 2009 CoreNet Global/Steelcase survey, 60% are using it for team spaces and 41% are reconfiguring to accommodate a wider variety of work and social settings such as cafes and meetings spaces.[12] Based on the study's findings, almost half of those surveyed are retaining a 1:1 ratio of people to seats. However, more of those seats are being located in settings outside of individual workstations. This means more flexible workplace solutions are being created.

"As millennials become more than 50 percent of the work force, the push for this work mode will only increase," predict Larsen and Rush.[10]

Individual Work Zones

Regardless of these new workplace solutions, it is still important for organizations to retain a balance of team spaces and places where individuals can perform heads-down, focused work. In a 2012 NeoCon seminar entitled, *You're Not Listening, I Need an Office,* Sven Govaars, a regional director for Gensler's consulting group, explained that employees' needs for quiet, individual work zones can easily be overshadowed by management's drive to reduce real estate and cost. "It's not about open vs. closed; it's more about how the office is going to function to support the culture of the organization and the individual," he said.[13]

Supporting Govaars' perception, 2011 research from Herman Miller, *Ws of Work: A Global Exploration on Collaboration,* revealed that people avoid 66% of so-called meeting spaces—designed to meet real estate efficiency and budgetary goals—because they don't meet their needs for quiet, private spaces so they can concentrate on their work.[14]

Encouraging corporations to better cater to worker preferences, Govaars claims that one fewer sick day per employee per year, or one extra hour of work per employee per week, can enable organizations to recoup a significant portion of their facility costs.[13]

Supporting this notion of better-designed workplace environments, Herman Miller has identified specific modes of work that workers engage in throughout the day. Researchers have labeled these modes as chat, cocreate, converse, divide and conquer, huddle, show and tell, warm up / cool down, process and respond, contemplate, and create. Based on these research findings, office furnishings can be developed to better support these various modes of work; meet behavior, cognitive, and physical criteria; and optimize worker productivity and organizational effectiveness.

In a 2014 workplace strategy report, CBRE lists some key steps to creating and supporting optimized work experiences:

- Create an aspiration with a clarity of focus and reasons why re-creating the work experience is worth the investment of time and resources.

- Map out the "touch points" between the individual and the organization, outlining the different ways in which the organization currently impacts the employee experience to provide a potentially better experience through technology, space, amenities, behavior, and culture.

• Consider the quality of experience that can potentially be created.

• Create an implementation plan where the gap between the current situation and the desired future situation is defined. In addition, identify what needs to change to achieve the desired outcome. Solutions can then be implemented incrementally, tested in pilots, or applied at scale in conjunction with other major business transformations.[4]

The Virtual Office

Although the workplace has been proven to maintain its relevance, particularly when set up to optimally support today's corporate culture, telecommuting and the virtual office remain major trends and important options.

One major variable driving a greater realization of virtual offices has been the development of the cloud platform—originally introduced by Amazon in 2006—enabling employees to store, access, and share data from a shared infrastructure platform supported by remote servers from anywhere in the world.

The rapid growth of Wi-Fi Internet connectivity in public and retail facilities is driving the new reality of working anywhere, anytime, in second or third places, and defined alternative workplaces such as home or the local coffee house. As defined by JLL, a third place is "a public area with club-like characteristics and a relaxed, comfortable atmosphere [that] offers networking opportunities and a less formal place for idea exchange that can benefit the business."[15] This might be a defined as a library, airport, or community center. Or more specifically, co-working centers—such as the Lower Manhattan Co-working Club—where freelancers, entrepreneurs, startups, and small businesses come together to use affordable, communal offices with a variety of workspaces and occasional programs and social events.

Mobile Work Requirements

To support increasing numbers of mobile workers, organizations—and particularly their IT departments—must address a number of newer requirements. Expectations and guidelines for mobile workers and distributed teams must be clearly established. This might mean guidebooks and websites where such guidelines, policies, and virtual procedures for security are specified, thereby legitimizing the company's mobile working program. For distributed teams, protocols for data sharing can be established along with formal structures that describe planned and spontaneous interactions.

Performance management agreements and remote training opportunities—including technology use, distributed work habits, and ergonomics—can be established. Mobile and distributed team workers can have access to a variety of software applications for collaboration, file sharing, virtual meetings, social networking, e-mail, instant messaging, document management, and tele-presence. IT can continue enhancing remote collaboration and virtual meeting capabilities. With all of the virtual collaboration and file sharing, organizations will need increased data storage, whether it's in the cloud or the data center.

Regarding mobile devices, such as smart phones and tablets, IT's policy on provisioning and supporting these devices should be made clear. There should also be clarity as to whether the company has standards on handheld devices or if there is support for a "bring your own device" program.

Of course, getting executive buy-in to implement these strategies is easier said than done. Experts recommend tailoring a business case to appeal to each management group. This can include calling out relevant metrics, measures, and processes that are pertinent to the proposed initiative. In addition, the business case should include "bulletproof financials" including external / internal costs, hard / soft costs, capital expenses, start-up and run-rate costs, and return on investment projections.

Workplace Productivity

New business challenges, evolving work patterns, and changes in today's corporate culture—including the demand for increased flexibility—

are causing shifts in corporate real estate portfolios for many companies. In response to these organizational changes, workplaces are being transformed to provide a variety of highly flexible work settings, offering choices to employees and addressing their well-being—all in the name of enhancing business results.

By considering the physical workplace when aligning business strategy and corporate culture, today's businesses seek to drive productivity and revenue, minimize costs, and improve employee retention. The success of these efforts will depend on a number of design aspects, including the physical environment of a workspace—its indoor air quality, lighting, and noise control—as well as design decisions for both individual and collaborative spaces.

A Changing Workspace Landscape

As discussed in previous chapters, business uncertainty, shifts in corporate cultures, and new work patterns have created the need for businesses and workplaces to demonstrate increased flexibility. Workers' appetites are growing for new workplace models, from revised office layouts to the provision of satellite and home offices. Simultaneously, an increased emphasis on corporate social responsibility has required that businesses engage in more sustainable practices, incorporating high-performance building design features that promote employee well-being. Together, these forces have altered the landscape of the corporate real estate portfolio, and they may promise increased productivity for companies that can successfully adapt.

According to a 2013 Gensler Consulting workplace report, 9 in 10 workers agreed that workplace design directly affects productivity, while 97% of employees experienced an increase in productivity due to telecommuting at least part-time during the week.[16] While all workplace programs are ultimately aimed at enhancing the operations, goals, and functions of the larger company, the most effective workplaces actively promote staff productivity through empowerment—offering choices of where to work and with whom. Flexible workplace design that includes key types of work—from individual to team and group work—provides a potential for enhanced performance both in and out of the office.

Measuring Workplace Productivity

Employee engagement is a key indicator in measuring workplace productivity, as engaged employees report lower turnover rates and lower absenteeism, while driving higher profits.[17] A 2014 Steelcase study across 14 countries revealed that the physical work environment has a strong impact on employee well-being and engagement. Because workplace productivity encompasses multiple factors that may vary from business to business and employee to employee, there is no single metric for its measurement. Generally, however, businesses have tools to track attendance and retention rates as well as direct costs and revenue; therefore, these metrics have become the basis for measuring workplace productivity today.

Attendance and Retention

Staff attendance and retention are connected to productivity because these indicators correlate with employee satisfaction and engagement as they relate to current job and office location. Happy employees are known to be twice as productive, to remain with their job five times longer, to use 10 times fewer sick days, to be three times more creative, and to achieve 37% higher sales.[16]

Committed and engaged employees who trust their management perform 20% better and are 87% less likely to leave an organization, resulting in easier employee and management recruitment, decreased training costs, and incalculable value in retained tenure equity. In addition, analysts indicate that the financial performance of publicly traded companies on the 100 Best Company List consistently outperform major stock indices by 300% and have half the voluntary turnover rates of their competitors.[18]

Research also shows that sustainably designed buildings can reduce absences related to illness while increasing productivity and employee engagement. Health and productivity costs imposed by poor indoor air quality in commercial buildings are estimated at nearly $100 billion USD annually. Employees working in sustainably designed environments report having 29% higher employee satisfaction and take between two and five fewer sick days annually.[1] Additionally, having the option to telecommute has been shown to reduce employee turnover. In fact, 59% of those who telecommute are less likely to look for another job.[16]

Costs and Revenue

Employee attendance and retention have a natural impact on the bottom line of any business. A company that retains its employees and keeps them healthy and focused will naturally spend less time and money on health care and hiring new recruits and temporary staff due to employee absences. In addition, when businesses allow telecommuting, they save an average of 33% during the first year due to real estate reductions and cost-per-person savings while also experiencing higher levels of employee satisfaction. About two-thirds of employees are happy with their flexible work programs.[19] Telecommuting has also been shown to reduce absenteeism costs by $2,000 USD annually per employee.[16]

Increased revenue is another byproduct of a happy and productive workforce. When employees are afforded workspace flexibility, revenue generation increases. According to a 2012 Regus study, as many as 68% of firms report that flexible working has led directly to increased revenue.[20] In that same study, 72% of global businesses report increased productivity as a direct result of flexible workplace practices. For example, teleworkers save as much as 91 minutes per day by not commuting to the office.[20]

Even small improvements in productivity can have significant impacts. For example, if an average U.S. company experienced a 4% increase in productivity among 80% of its employees, it would see a $1.5 million USD annual boost. Simply achieving a $1 USD increase in productivity per employee per year would allow the company to recoup the costs of running their facilities.[16]

Environmental Impacts:
Air, Natural Lighting, and Noise Control

While we've learned that telecommuting can be a significant force behind employee satisfaction, there are situations when employees must be present in the corporate office, such as for face-to-face meetings, when a project team is at the beginning of a work cycle, or when team members are newer and establishing relationships, to name a few. Similarly, some job functions make telecommuting difficult or altogether impossible. Therefore, thoughtful workplace design remains a powerful tool in supporting optimal employee performance. In fact, 9 out of 10 employees believe that workplace design affects their productivity.[16]

But which workplace design strategies are key to heightened productivity? The most significant variables include: air (thermal comfort and temperature), natural lighting (access to views and daylight), and acoustics (noise control).[21]

Air

Achieving the right combination of thermal comfort, which must take into account temperature, airflow, and humidity, can be complex. According to a 2013 HOK report, one key to thermal comfort is maintaining the ideal temperature of 70.88°F in an office environment. In fact, research has demonstrated that for every 1.8°F change in temperature (up or down), there is a 1% to 2% decrease in performance.[21]

The climate and location of the building and its local environmental qualities will determine the most applicable strategies for promoting indoor air quality in the building. According to HOK, organizations seeking to promote comfortable spaces with optimal indoor air quality may want to consider the following strategies:

- Utilize an underfloor air distribution system, which provides individual control of airflow and better space delivery of air;

- Implement zone temperature controls /or provide individual controls in enclosed spaces;

- Install operable windows to maximize sunlight, airflow, and temperature control where weather permits; and

- Specify interior furnishings with low or no volatile organic compounds.[21]

Natural Lighting

A study by Herman Miller and Claremont Graduate University demonstrated that participants experienced elevated moods and increased their creative problem-solving ability in spaces with daylight and views.[22]

The study posits that when employees are surrounded by natural views and daylight, they are happier and can be more productive. Because daylight helps regulate the daily cycle of waking and sleeping hours, the presence of daylight and windows whenever possible in the office environment can positively impact employee well-being and promote productivity. Organizations can implement the following strategies to enhance daylight and views:

- Organize the space to maximize natural light penetration into the interior areas of the floor, which can include locating enclosed spaces at the building's core and open spaces at its perimeter;

- Use transparent glass whenever possible and opaque glass where visual privacy is required; and

- Place shared spaces with access to the best views.[21]

Noise Control

Noise control is an issue in most office environments, and controlling it can be a significant challenge, depending on the facility's function and the end business product. In 2011, the U.S. General Services Administration published a guide to workplace acoustics, noting that office acoustics are "a key contributor to work performance and wellbeing in the workplace. The ability to find quiet time and places is essential to supporting complex knowledge work. Acoustical comfort is achieved when the workplace provides appropriate acoustical support for interaction, confidentiality and concentrative work."[21]

The following steps can help mitigate the negative effects of unwanted noise in the workplace:

- Utilize materials that promote noise absorption, blocking, and sound masking, including furniture, acoustical ceilings, fabrics, carpet, walls, and partitions;

- Design the workplace in a way that separates noisier spaces from quieter work areas as much as possible; and

- Group employees by work pattern or department, in open plenum offices.[21]

Design Implications

Increased support for workplace flexibility has given employees more options for where they work and therefore had an effect on the way space is used within the total corporate office footprint. The total space allotted to individual work spaces and private offices has been reduced, while the real estate dedicated to collaborative spaces has grown, reflecting an increased value placed on collaboration by most companies today.

New trends in both individual and collaborative spaces have emerged as a result. The large corporate boardroom has been upstaged by smaller meeting rooms, and open office space is now being repurposed for smaller work stations, intended to foster collaboration and promote productivity. All in all, corporate office designs that have accompanied the evolving model of work have changed the face of corporate real estate portfolios all over the world.

Individual Spaces

Employees generally need the opportunity to work in a variety of places—from collaborative to private. More recently, workplace design has focused on ways to create privacy in typically open offices. As a result, many companies now provide a collection of diverse work settings that offer choice and control in terms of managing distractions and information security. These solutions can include phone booths or small, private areas meant to be used for "head-down tasks." In fact, in a 2011 Knoll study, as many as 20% of the organizations surveyed (40 organizations from 11 industries, representing a variety of business models and worldwide locations) provided only open work areas or touchdown stations without any enclosed offices, while half of the organizations with private offices deemed them unassigned—to be used by any employee as needed.[19]

Collaborative Spaces

Today's average corporate boardroom isn't as large or formal as it once was. Instead, collaborative spaces are now typically smaller in size, and rooms that hold between two to seven people typically have utilization rates that are 20% higher than meetings rooms designed for eight or more persons. [19]

A variety of collaborative spaces, both in size and seating type, are now offered across today's corporate real estate portfolios. These can include enclosed project areas with small tables, e-cafés for small-group meetings, and open office settings that provide a backdrop for serendipitous collaboration. Yesterday's large conference rooms are now being repurposed as war rooms, project rooms, or agile team rooms with new, flexible furniture that can be reconfigured to reflect the needs of its occupants.

Conclusion

Mobility trends, changing demographics, and varying expectations have created a pressing need for organizations to adapt their workplace environment. This means organizations must address the need for flexible workspaces, increased support for mobile workers, and a greater focus on the work / life balance.

In order to truly maximize productivity and enhance employee satisfaction, companies must carefully study and assess their staff's working styles and preferences, and then build up their work environment, resources, and tools to optimally support these styles. Creating this new workplace environment will allow companies to recruit more easily and retain the top talent that is essential for a company to meet and potentially exceed its goals.

Because there is a strong correlation between a high-performing workplace and a high-performing workforce, companies are beginning to shift their office interiors and work practices to incorporate increased flexibility. The goal is to leverage the workplace to support the development of a thriving employee base. When key workplace elements, such as air quality, lighting, and noise control are improved while flexibility and collaboration are emphasized, it is possible for corporate real estate portfolios to increase employee productivity. Changes in revenue and employee retention rates often directly follow changes to the physical workplace and its practices—having a direct impact on productivity.

References

1. Mladenova, I., & Gresty, M. (2012, July/August). Alternative workplace strategies: Building the case. *The Leader*. Retrieved from https://resources.corenetglobal.org/knowledgecenteronline/SearchByTopicAndResource.aspx?ID=3275

2. Lister, K., & Harnish, T. (2011). *State of telework in the U.S.* Global Workplace Analytics. Retrieved from http://www.workshifting.com/downloads/downloads/Telework-Trends-US.pdf

3. CoreNet Global. (2012). *Corporate real estate 2020*. Retrieved from http://www.corenet-global.org/Publications/content.cfm?ItemNumber=15836

4. CBRE. (2014). *Workplace strategy: Why one size does not fit all*. CBRE, Asia Pacific Special Report. Available from http://www.cbre.com/EN/research/asia%20pacific%20research/specialreports/Pages/Workplace-Strategy-One-size-does-not-fit-all.aspx

5. Gensler. (2013). *2013 U.S. workplace survey: Key findings*. Retrieved from http://www.gensler.com/uploads/documents/2013_US_Workplace_Survey_07_15_2013.pdf

6. Harter, J., & Agrawal, S. (2014, Jan. 20). *Many Baby Boomers reluctant to retire*. Gallup. Retrieved from http://www.gallup.com/poll/166952/baby-boomers-reluctant-retire.aspx

7. U.S. Department of Labor. (2010). *Employment Report*. Bureau of Labor Statistics. Retrieved from http://www.bls.gov/home.htm

8. Creating Corporate Value. (2014, August). MCR class. Slide 21 of 25.

9. Heerwagen, J., Anderson, D., & Porter, W. (2012). *NetWork: The Future Workplace*. AndersonPorter Design, J. H. Heerwagen. Retrieved from https://resources.corenetglobal.org/knowledgecenteronline/SearchByTopicAndResource.aspx?ID=6713

10. Larsen, R., & Rush, S. (2012, March/April). A generation ahead: Strategic real estate planning guide for tomorrow's work force. *The Leader*. Retrieved from http://s3.amazonaws.com/sph-1/news/185/original/Norman%20Partners%20article.pdf

11. CoreNet Global. (2012). *Corporate real estate 2020 final report: Workplace*. Retrieved from https://resources.corenetglobal.org/knowledgecenteronline/SearchByTopicAndResource.aspx?ID=4423

12. Kadzis, R. (2009, September/October). CoreNet Global/Steelcase research findings: Reducing the portfolio and maximizing existing space. *The Leader*. Retrieved from http://www.nxtbook.com/nxtbooks/corenet/theleader0909/index.php?startid=66

13. Govaars, S. (2012). *You're not listening: I need an office*. Presentation at NeoCon 2012. Retrieved from https://resources.corenetglobal.org/knowledgecenteronline/SearchByTopicAndResource.aspx?ID=5966

14. Herman Miller. (2011). *Ws of Work: A Global Exploration on Collaboration*.

15. Jones Lang LaSalle. (2008, November). *Perspectives on workplace*.

16. Govaars, S. (2013, September/October). The value of human capital. *The Leader*. Retrieved from https://resources.corenetglobal.org/knowledgecenteronline/SearchBy-TopicAndResource.aspx?ID=1984

17. Moutrey, G. (2014). Power of place: The office renaissance. *Steelcase 360 Magazine*, issue 68. Retrieved from http://www.steelcase.com/insights/articles/power-of-place/

18. Great Place to Work Institute. (2015). *Identifying best places to work*. Retrieved from http://www.greatplacetowork.com/best-companies

19. O'Neill, M., & Wymer, T. D. (2011). The metrics of distributed work: Financial and performance benefits of an emerging work model. *Knoll Workplace Research*. Retrieved from https://resources.corenetglobal.org/knowledgecenteronline/SearchBy-TopicAndResource.aspx?ID=1882

20. Regus. (2012). *Flexibility drives productivity*. Retrieved from https://resources.corenet-global.org/knowledgecenteronline/SearchByTopicAndResource.aspx?ID=593

21. Stringer, L. (2013). *Workplace strategies that enhance human performance, health and wellness*. HOK. Retrieved from https://resources.corenetglobal.org/knowledgecen-teronline/SearchByTopicAndResource.aspx?ID=1935

22. Herman Miller, Inc. (2014). *The neurophysiology of office design study: The objective findings*. Retrieved from http://mem-events.com/newsfuse/uploads/documents/2015-Mar/40-The-Neurophysiology-of-Office-Design.pdf

Chapter 14

Business Continuity

Summary

Business continuity has been defined as the process by which companies mitigate, to the greatest extent possible, unacceptable risks to their commercial viability, taking all reasonable and prudent measures to ensure that the company's critical operations will continue to function throughout any emergency and, in the unlikely event that they are unable to do so, that they can be restored to operational capacity as quickly and seamlessly as possible.[1]

Business continuity has evolved from an IT-centric process to a holistic risk management discipline to ensure the continued operational or commercial viability of corporations, institutions and government agencies alike. It encompasses a wide range of functions: IT, HR, manufacturing, finance, marketing and more. Since all those activities are conducted in corporate real property assets, business continuity has far-reaching implications for corporate real estate professionals.

The Sept. 11, 2001, terrorist attacks on New York City and Washington, D.C., were a watershed event in the evolution of business continuity. When global financial services and other companies were forced to suspend operations in Lower Manhattan following the attacks, business leaders realized that their capacity to operate during times of emergency or disaster depended on far more than their IT infrastructure. They realized they were also dependent on the availability of their work force, their ability to communicate (to customers, staff, vendors, the public, and government) and access to their real estate and facilities.

Business continuity as it pertains to corporate real estate has two fundamental principles:

- Unacceptable risks to a property's operational availability during adverse circumstances must be identified and, if possible, mitigated.

- Plans, procedures and protocols must be established to enable real estate and facilities professionals to react immediately and effectively to any emergency situation to ensure the ongoing availability of the property and, in a worst-case scenario, to restore the property to operational status as quickly as possible.

This chapter is divided into three sections that provide an introduction and overview of key business continuity principles and practices. Section one begins with a brief history of the business continuity discipline and discusses its growing importance across the corporate enterprise. Section two describes the critical elements involved in developing a business continuity program. Section three offers a relevant case study that provides insights and lessons learned from a real world business continuity event.

History of Business Continuity

The business continuity discipline is relatively new but quickly maturing. In just the past two decades, the discipline has undergone a full paradigm shift within the corporate sector—evolving from an often reactive, limited-scope "disaster responder" to a proactive, globally integrated monitor and maintainer of critical business operations.

Modern business continuity programs emerged in the 1960s as organizations entered an era of automated processing and sought to develop holistic response plans that moved beyond the standard "life safety" plans in place. Managers of this era understood the benefits of backing up critical records and processes; however, there was no consistent standard being applied to these efforts.

In the 1970s and 1980s, the explosive growth of computer systems motivated many businesses to assess their operations and pursue wider strategies to identify and protect the growing information, technology, and telecommunications networks that had become so critical to their business. As a direct correlation, leading organizations of this era began taking focused steps to mitigate the potential damage that could be caused by unforeseen gaps within increasingly interconnected and dispersed operations. Their actions led to the development of the industry's first formalized "disaster recovery" plans.

Through the 1990s and 2000s, globalization and automation continued at lightning pace while organizations increased in size and global presence, putting their operations at greater risk to both natural and manmade disasters. Given the growing interdependence of global businesses, reverberating and potentially long-term damages now were not only possible but expected—even well outside a localized area of immediate impact. This escalating vulnerability drove a new C-level priority: the development of robust business continuity management (BCM) programs that promote a more resilient and continually operable business model.

Today's business continuity professionals face the added challenge of a 24/7 news cycle. This prospect of heightened media scrutiny has further motivated many organizations to invest in business continuity management programs as they seek to assure their clients and shareholders that they possess resilient and rapidly recoverable business models. In fact, an organization's continuity capabilities have now become a strong indicator of overall organizational stability, and business continuity management has the potential to positively influence employees, clients, and investors during a pivotal time of great organizational need and heightened media exposure.

This realization has motivated many organizations to ensure their continuity programs are proactively planned, clearly structured, and resilient. As a result, today's business continuity management program leaders now plan against a matrix of all possible hazards, providing organization-spanning plans and capabilities to effectively protect, promptly respond, and efficiently recover critical operations—regardless of what events or circumstances an organization may face.

As the business continuity management process has matured, professionals within corporate real estate organizations were first called upon to contribute to growing continuity and response teams. This was due largely to their traditional roles and unique capabilities in facility management. Today, as professionals from multiple lines of business shoulder continuity responsibilities across the portfolio, many corporate real estate professionals have found themselves with expanded responsibilities—often serving as either an integrator or leader for these enterprise-wide operations.

Developing a Business Continuity Management Program

This section outlines the overarching structure and critical components that organizations should consider when either evaluating or developing a business continuity management program.

It is important to note a key delineation: corporate business continuity management programs are enterprise-wide operations that drive an organization's continuity planning and response operations. They inform event-driven and situation-specific business continuity plans (BCPs), which are planning documents used to prepare and guide an organization's response effort. While there is often a single business continuity management program, multiple business continuity plans will usually be drafted to provide details about how to effectively respond to a wide array of continuity events.

Events that trigger a business continuity management response are most often complex, fast-moving, and extremely taxing to an organization. Accordingly, having a robust, resilient, and realistic business continuity management program in place before such an event occurs has become a strategic priority for leading organizations—as well as a requirement when operating in certain high-risk areas and business sectors.

As outlined by the Business Continuity Institute, a membership and certification organization for business continuity professionals worldwide, the core life cycle of an organization's business continuity management program should include the four key areas listed below.[2]

- Understanding the organization
- Determining the business continuity management strategy
- Developing and implementing a business continuity management response
- Exercising, maintaining, and reviewing

Understanding the Organization

Business continuity management plans are typically developed by steering committees comprised of C-level executives, who establish organizational expectations and program goals; business line leaders from HR, finance, risk management, technology, health, safety, and environment (HSE), procurement, and corporate real estate, among others, who provide subject matter expertise; and experienced business continuity professionals, who guide the committee through the necessary stages, best practices, and requirements of the work ahead.

The steering committee establishes the organization's business continuity strategy. Drawing upon their collective experience with the organization, committee members must first describe and document the state of the organization as it operates under normal conditions, then describe and document the state of the organization as it intends to respond to hypothetical continuity scenarios. This process includes envisioning the critical needs, resources, and outcomes throughout these scenarios. The top priorities for the steering committee include developing, overseeing, and supporting the following program elements, according to the National Fire Protection Association (2009):[3]

- The policies, plans, and procedures to develop, implement, and maintain the business continuity management program

- Resources to support the program

- Review processes and evaluations to ensure program effectiveness

- Correction of deficiencies

Determining the Business Continuity Management Strategy

The foundation of a resilient business continuity management program is a clear strategy that will establish an organization's approach and provide the organizational parameters to guide future actions. This strategy should provide details on how resources are to be engaged across the enterprise and how they will be used to develop any requisite future policies and capabilities, maintaining close adherence to the steering committee's founding goals and principles.

Once the strategy is in place, policy documents must be developed to clearly outline the program's scope and framework of operations. At a minimum, these documents should provide details on business continuity management accountable parties, planning requirements, maintenance and testing schedules, and operational requirements. The scope of a business continuity management policy should cover all lines of business, corporate subsidiaries, and critical vendors with responsibilities to assist in continuity operations.

The scope of a business continuity management policy often can be limited by factors such as diverse products and services, locations, availability of resources, and organizational culture.[3] Therefore, it is important for the organization to take a risk-based approach in its assessment, ensuring the limited resources dedicated to this effort are focused on the most critical business processes. The policy should be transparent and clearly communicated to all parties involved—those who may be impacted as well as those who may be responding—to ensure coordination during the response and recovery time period.

Once a business continuity management strategy and initial policies have been established, a business impact analysis (BIA) should be performed.[2] Business impact analyses are formally structured procedures that provide the framework for a holistic assessment and mapping of an organization's operational risks, criticalities, and recovery priorities.

At minimum, according to the *BSI Standards Publication* (p. 15),[4] the business impact analysis should:

- Identify activities that support the organization's operations, products, and services;

- Assess the impacts over time of not performing these activities;

- Set prioritized time frames for resuming these activities at a specified minimum acceptable level, taking into consideration at what point in time the impact of not resuming the activities would become unacceptable; and

- Identify dependencies and supporting resources for these activities, including suppliers, outsource partners, and other relevant interested parties.

The results of the impact analysis will help the organization prioritize actions and steer the future direction of the program's development. With the impact analysis complete and the initial potential for impacts and priorities established, the business continuity management team should next commence an operational "risk assessment" to identify all sources of risk and potential impacts to critical organizational processes. These risks may be due to natural, societal, cultural, political, financial or general business disruptions. A thorough risk assessment should be designed and executed to:

- Identify risks of disruption to the organization's prioritized activities and the processes, systems, information, people, assets, outsource partners, and other resources that support them;

- Systematically analyze risk;

- Evaluate which disruptions and related risks require treatment; and

- Identify treatments commensurate with business continuity objectives and in accordance with the organization's risk appetite (*BSI Standards Publication*, p. 16).[4]

Together, the business impact analysis and risk assessment will help to identify, list, and rank business processes by criticality of operation and priority of future address. Once complete, the analysis team will have an adequate mapping of key current state operations, known areas of need, and weighted measurements for potential starting points of future work.

Developing and Implementing a Business Continuity Management Response

The magnitude, scope, and urgency of an organization's business continuity management response will depend on the specific circumstances of the initiating event. Despite this high potential for variability, responses should strive for consistency by incorporating these elements: a standardized response team structure, a communications protocol, required response times, and a plan for process recovery. The actions required for each of these elements are explored further here.

Standardize the response team structure. Developing a formal crisis management team (CMT) is necessary to allow the organization a proactive and coordinated response. A crisis management team ensures a predetermined team is responsible and ready to activate all proper personnel and resources to execute plans and commence a thorough response and recovery effort. While incident specifics will mandate the team's final composition, a recommended structure includes:

Team leader/incident commander. Leads the team and acts as the "decision maker" regarding activating business continuity plans, acquiring resources, and setting the overall recovery strategy.

Line of business leaders. Provides structure to link normal operations to the crisis management team decision set, ensuring all requirements are properly communicated and implemented at the departmental level.

Business continuity team. Determines which plans and protocols to invoke and coordinates with the business to determine impact or assistance required.

Risk management. Manages and advises the insurance assessment and claims process for potential claims.

Health, safety, and environmental. Ensures adherence to all safety standards and oversees the check-and-balance measures to ensure staff safety remains the top priority for recovery.

Corporate communications. Provides expertise on the development and distribution of information both internally and externally, ensuring compliance with corporate policies and protection of the company from unauthorized information disclosures.

Information technology. Ensures impacts to the IT infrastructure can properly be mitigated to cause minimal impact to recovery strategies.

Colleagues and contractors representing specific departments and lines of business can always be added to or removed from the crisis management team. Given the scope of their work, professionals from risk management, corporate security, legal and compliance, and HR, are a natural fit. Of note, whenever a business continuity management program includes a critical scope of work outsourced to an external organization, a direct line of communication should be established and maintained with the provider before, throughout, and following a business continuity management activation whenever possible.

Establish the communications protocol. A critical aspect in the planning process is providing certainty and awareness in crisis communications. Crisis communications should be uniformly structured to ensure consistency in form, content, and delivery across communication channels. These messages should be planned for release at predetermined intervals established in the business continuity management planning phase (i.e., immediately following, within 15 minutes, 24 hours following, etc.). A crisis communication protocol should clearly delineate the status of incident, any known impacts to the organization, all actions taken to date, and the crisis management team's next steps / actions planned.[5]

Ensuring employee safety is the primary concern for an organization seeking to recover from a continuity event. Effective means of communicating with employees and obtaining employee status updates are numerous yet increasingly trending toward Emergency Mass Notification Systems (EMNS) that automate the outreach process and can sync traditional communications devices (i.e., phones, laptops, tablets) with business continuity management-specific tools and technology. As a hedge against potential impact and response readiness, business continuity management tools and resources can be virtually and/or physically located away from core company environments (i.e., off-site or with a third party).

Determine response time requirements. Predetermined response times should be established for all critical business processes and applications identified in the business impact analysis. Integral to the impact analysis, the business continuity management team should work with business unit leaders to identify and determine three key timetables matching their internal and external business requirements:

Maximum tolerable period of disruption (MTPD) determines the maximum time an organization can be impacted before financial or reputational viability are irreparably damaged.[2]

Recovery time objective (RTO) is the period of time within which an individual process must be recovered or resumed.[4]

Recovery Point Objective (RPO) is the point when information used by an activity must be restored.[4]

Identifying these three objectives guides the process recovery steps to ensure a successful process recovery occurs before the incident seriously impacts a corporation's future ability to conduct normal business operations.

Plan for process recovery. Process recovery planning is defined in multiple ways within the business continuity profession; however, all definitions incorporate strategies to recover from a full or partial loss of:

- Facility or premises (typically due to physical damage to facility or utilities);

- Technology or equipment (typically due to loss of technology connectivity or loss damage of critical equipment);

- People / employees (typically due to pandemic situations, labor union issues, or civil actions and protests); and

- Critical third-party vendors (typically due to contracting issues, failure of third-party suppliers).

Business continuity plans should account for each scenario and should be developed in a manner that allows for sufficient flexibility to ensure that resources can be redirected to assess and address the most critical needs. The amount of continuity planning assigned to this matrix initiative will depend entirely upon the level of risk an organization is willing to accept.

Exercising, Maintaining, and Reviewing the Business Continuity Plan

Persistent maintenance and testing of the business continuity management program is crucial to its continued success. At minimum, the business continuity policy and framework should include an annual maintenance cycle for the program. Depending on the criticality of systems protected and the level of your business continuity management program, testing may be set at any time period up to and including real-time continual monitoring and evaluations. Testing will provide a dual purpose of training team members as well as verifying recovery processes in situations that approximate real-world events. Subsequent business continuity plan updates should include any recognized changes to processes, technology, team members, or equipment.

Testing of business continuity plans can occur at multiple levels of complexity and scope, including the three common methods shown below.[2]

Plan walkthrough. Plan owners and users review planning together to ensure process steps are accurate and relevant.

Table-top exercise. One or more plans are reviewed concurrently based upon a simulated incident.

Full exercise (also referred to as "war-gaming"). This is a simulated incident with the crisis management and business continuity planning teams required to respond to a continuity event and to implement their strategies and process steps to respond and recover accordingly.

It is prudent to review and update business continuity plans following all business continuity management activations. Lessons learned from the incident response can be logged into an "after action report" with tasks and timetables assigned to update plans and/or modify operational processes.

Case Study: Superstorm Sandy

No amount of planning can replace the lessons learned from responding to a real-world event. As such, the following case study is offered as an example of a thorough business continuity management planning, response, and recovery operation.

Event

Superstorm Sandy has often been referred to as the largest Atlantic hurricane on record. The storm made landfall in October 2012, coming ashore with winds above 90 miles per hour, heavy rains, and a historic storm swell. The storm caused 159 deaths, affected 24 states, and damaged more than 650,000 homes and 300,000 businesses. New York, Connecticut, and New Jersey were particularly hard hit, experiencing long-term power outages, communication and transportation interruptions, major flooding, and extensive structural damage. Sandy is estimated to have caused at least $65 billion USD in damages.

Business Continuity Management Response

Before the storm hit, knowing that hundreds of client locations were within the storm's projected path, CBRE's global business continuity management team launched business continuity management operations and began communicating with clients and colleagues to activate regional, client, and location-specific business continuity plans in concert with the storm notifications being transmitted by the National Weather Service. Led by a crisis management team incident commander, CBRE engaged the company's engineers, technicians, facility managers, project managers, contracting officers, global risk management, and health, safety, and environmental team members into a well-tested preparation and response structure.

Working with hundreds of clients, contractors, and colleagues, the business continuity management team implemented thorough business continuity plans to quickly align and launch operations to protect, mitigate damage to, and recover client real estate assets within all determined time frames. Their actions included a prioritized site assessment and facility reinforcement initiative before the storm hit; around-the-clock security and on-demand building repair for critical systems and facilities (including multiple grid-to-generator power switches) during the storm; and site assessment and repair, vacancy identification, and new workspace construction initiatives after the storm.

The business continuity management plans that had been developed and tested over the years, including several days just prior to landfall, were instrumental in mitigating losses, restoring services, and reopening client facilities to meet or exceed all predetermined time tables. Highlights of the team's responses included:

- Mobilizing 3,500 man-hours of labor from as far away as Florida and Texas—all focused on protecting and assessing client sites, commencing restoration efforts, and relieving impacted staff.

- Contracting private fuel tankers to deliver 46,000 gallons of fuel to power critical facilities and vehicles (hospitals and ambulances included) at the heart of the response.

- Activating global alert lines and an advanced operations center that provided a defined entry point and response capability for saving lives and facilities and stabilizing operations before, during, and after the storm.

- Launching a customized disaster recovery webpage focused on aligning and integrating thousands of global staff and vendors to carry out Superstorm Sandy response and recovery initiatives.

- Providing connectivity across all impacted client accounts—opening lines of communication and leveraging a unique capability to shift key resources (i.e., generators, technicians, specialized vendor contracts) among impacted entities to meet peaks and valleys in facility specific demands.

- Providing twice-daily business continuity management incident alert updates summarizing the holistic corporate response. These communications kept executive leaders current on enterprise-wide issues and served as a touch point for the crisis management team to convene and discuss specific action items needed to support an effective and efficient response.

Lessons Learned

Superstorm Sandy tested the organizational stamina and continuity capabilities across more than 300,000 impacted businesses. In several cases, losses were inevitable due to the historic scale and breadth of storm damage. In many cases, however, organizational commitment and investment in business continuity management became readily apparent through affected organizations' ability to maintain either continuous uptime or minimize downtime in their operations.

In the case of CBRE, advance business continuity management planning and testing prepared both client and contracted organizations to effectively partner and communicate and to conduct vital operations in the most challenging of environments. Lessons learned demonstrate the vital need to:

- Quickly establish and communicate an organization's incident commander, all status reporting tools and formats, and clear protocols for decision requests, escalation, and execution.

- Provide clear access to a centralized call center charged with aggregating field requests, directing solutions across the portfolio (e.g., fuel supply contracts), monitoring open items, and addressing rapidly emerging needs.

- Maintain rigorous testing, training, and after-action reporting to ensure employees and clients are readily familiar with all business continuity management personnel, processes, procedures, and technologies prior to a continuity event.

Information Sources

This chapter offers a primer on the business continuity management discipline. Readers interested in learning more on this topic are encouraged to review the industry standards and governing bodies. These documents provide a clear next step for any organization seeking knowledge and guidance on implementing or improving a business continuity program.

ISO 22301. ISO (International Organization for Standardization) is a worldwide federation that works to prepare and carry out international standards. This document provides industry standards for establishing and managing an effective business continuity management system.

NFPA 1600. NFPA (National Fire Protection Association) develops standards on disaster and emergency management, including business continuity. This document establishes a common set of criteria for managing an all-hazards disaster or emergency. It provides the fundamental criteria to develop, implement, assess, and maintain the program for prevention, mitigation, preparedness, response, continuity, and recovery.

Business Continuity Institute's *Good Practice Guidelines.* The Business Continuity Institute convenes senior practitioners who have developed and shaped the concept of Business Continuity internationally. *Good Practice Guidelines* (GPG) is intended for practitioners, consultants, auditors, and regulators with a working knowledge of the rationale for business continuity management and its basic principles.

ASIS SPC.1–2009. The American Society for Industrial Security developed a series of resilience standards to address the risks of disruptive events. Using a balance of adaptive, proactive, and reactive strategies, these five activities offer a holistic, business-friendly approach to risk and resilience management. This document provides a framework for businesses to assess the risks of disruptive events, develop a proactive strategy, establish performance criteria, and evaluate opportunities for improvement.

ASIS BSI business continuity management.1–2010. The standard developed by American Society for Industrial Security provides auditable criteria with accompanying guidance for developing and implementing a business continuity management system. BSI is a leading global provider of risk-based solutions, assessments and training programs.

Conclusion

Most large corporations have well-developed business continuity programs that encompass corporate real estate, but some may not. Corporate real estate professionals can lower their company's risk profile by ensuring that real estate and facilities are integrated into the corporate business continuity program, if one exists.

If no such company-wide program is in place, corporate real estate leaders can develop their own business continuity plan to ensure that the corporation's mission-critical facilities remain operational during an emergency or disaster.

References

1. Rosenbluth, J. (2011, September/October). The Evolution of Business Continuity and Risk Management: What Are the Implications for Corporate Occupiers? *The Leader*. Retrieved from https://resources.corenetglobal.org/knowledgecenteronline/Search-ByTopicAndResource.aspx?ID=3163

2. Bird, L., editor. (2010). *The Business Continuity Institute good practice guidelines* (global ed.). Retrieved from http://www.thebci.org/index.php/resources/the-good-practice-guidelines

3. National Fire Protection Association. (2009). *NFPA 1600: Standard on disaster/emergency management and business continuity programs*. Quincy, MA: Author.

4. International Organization for Standardization. (2012). *BSI standards publication. ISO 22301:2012 societal security: Business continuity management systems—requirements*.

5. CBRE Business Continuity Management. (2015). *CBRE global crisis management standards document* (vers. 2.0).

Chapter 15

Internal Partnering

Summary

As multiple pressures bear down on today's corporations—constrained budgets, the difficulties of attracting and retaining talent, the need to adopt sustainable practices—the organization's infrastructure and support services are expected to perform more efficiently and in more innovative ways.

In order to tap into this core group's hidden potential, significantly deeper forms of collaboration and integration must be established across the organization. A highly integrated shared services organization can help companies reach this goal.

Highly Integrated Shared Services Organizations

A highly integrated shared services organization is a newer hierarchical structure where key departments—namely corporate real estate, information technology (IT), finance, and human resources (HR)—collaborate to integrate relationship management, planning, systems and strategy for support functions.

Numerous studies have found shared services organizations can achieve cost savings, efficiencies, and better service. A 2011 Accenture study, *Trends in Shared Services: Unlocking the Full Potential*, shows that many companies have merely scratched the surface of the potential impact as they employ a limited shared service structure that contributes little to the company's overarching strategic objectives.[1]

CoreNet Global's research report, *Corporate Real Estate 2020: Partnering with Key Support Functions,* states, "for a shared service organization to evolve, a company must move beyond the basic infrastructure and service consolidation to create a true intersection of collaborating support functions that is empowered to drive and develop strategy that not only enables the business, but impacts all support functions."[2]

According to Kathleen A. Murphy, an agency dispute resolution specialist with the U.S. Defense Logistics Agency, partnering:

- Encourages different organizations to work together to attain the desired result instead of engaging in finger-pointing whenever problems occur;

- Helps eliminate surprises that can lead to delays and additional costs through increased communications; and

- Avoids conflict by establishing informal resolution management procedures, allowing all parties to anticipate and resolve problems before they become formal conflicts.[3]

Two-thirds of survey respondents in the CoreNet Global Corporate Real Estate 2020 research predict that organizations will adopt highly integrated shared services organizations by 2020 as a means to support a more productive workforce.[2]

Role of Corporate Real Estate Professionals

With key input from these various entities within an organization, all decisions—from real estate acquisition to telework policies to interior design—can be made in ways that best support the company and lead to increased efficiencies, cost reductions, and greater satisfaction among employees. Because corporate real estate leaders already regularly interact with the company's assorted support functions, they are well-versed at maneuvering between multiple executives while managing complex projects. Thus, corporate real estate professionals can help organizations take the first step toward creating a highly integrated shared services organization.

"Corporate real estate executives have a unique opportunity to assume new leadership roles based on core competency project management skills and their valuable experience in integrating HR, IT and other support functions for large-scale projects," according to the CoreNet Global 2020 report.[2]

This process is best accepted when it is gradually implemented into the daily course of business. The implementation of an integrated shared services organization can be hampered by internal politics and resistance to change; in order to succeed, silos must be broken down so that limited resources can be deployed to create the new organizational structure. Additional hurdles may include integrating systems and processes across diverse functional areas, dealing with an inflexible supplier base, finding capital to launch, and locating the necessary resources to support the highly integrated shared services organization. By utilizing change management practices, many of these obstacles can be removed.

A large percentage of organizations do appear to be moving toward the highly integrated shared services organization model. A 2011 Deloitte Consulting survey found that more than 90% of companies are implementing various iterations of shared services structures.[4]

Current Models

The Corporate Real Estate 2020 report lays out four current models of highly integrated shared services organizations:

- Ad hoc

- Functional and project-based

- Partially integrated around business units

- Fully integrated across the enterprise[2]

As stated in a CoreNet Global publication, "Partnering with Key Support Functions," high-performance corporations are expected to put greater demand on their infrastructure and services in order to remain competitive in the marketplace.[5] To do so, deeper forms of collaboration between enterprise support functions will be necessary. Necessary prerequisites to drive this dramatic change in the executive structure are top-down leadership and a desire for cultural alignment.

Emergence of New Integrated Workplace Leadership

Part and parcel of the highly integrated shared services organization model is an enhanced central leadership group with strong strategic planning skills, a deep understanding of the business, and wide exposure to other support functions.

A 2011 CoreNet Global/CBRE "upskilling" survey found that four of the five most important skills for corporate real estate groups are "soft" business skills: relationship building, strategic thinking, cross-functional collaboration, and change management.[6] Furthermore, more than half of the respondents who rated strategic thinking and change management as high in importance reported that their own team lacked those skills.

However, almost three-quarters of all professionals surveyed in the CoreNet Global Corporate Real Estate 2020 study anticipate that this integrated workplace leadership will be in place by the year 2020. Within this evolving leadership model, corporate real estate executives will be increasingly relied upon more for their strategic and business acumen than for their traditional real estate and facilities skills.[2] According to the study, a number of organizations plan to bridge this gap between leadership, business acumen, and real estate skills with organizational changes, outsourcing strategies, training plans, and a skills shift for the customer relationship managers.

To provide an idea of what integrated leadership looks like, a 2012 *The Leader* article, "Partnering with Key Support Functions," highlights Procter & Gamble's global business services unit.[5] By successfully integrating IT, finance, facilities, procurement, and other shared service entities into one leadership group, P&G documented savings of more than $900 million USD from 2003 to 2011 and cut costs as a percent of sales by one-third.

With its integrated resource model, P&G was much better equipped to improve quality, innovation, and productivity while simultaneously lowering costs. For example, the deployment of video collaboration studios by global business services saved $4 USD in travel costs for every $1 USD invested.

The Shortcoming of Silos

When corporate real estate, facilities management, HR, and IT operate independently of one another, these silos fall short of delivering enterprise value, noted Larry Barkley, Kyra Cavanaugh, and Gary Miciunas in a 2012 white paper, *Flex Work: A Collaborative Model for FM, HR & IT.*[7]

For example, corporate real estate management is tasked with improving space utilization and reducing occupancy cost, so the department is well-positioned to encourage telecommuting. However, it exerts no control over purchasing and setting up the technologies to enable this change. Meanwhile, the information technology department is more concerned about managing security and reliability, so supporting mobile workers may not be high on its priority list. And while human resources would like to promote flex work to boost recruiting and retention, they lack the corporate real estate and information technology resources to make it happen. Improved communication and tighter-knit relationships could help resolve these issues.

"Collectively, synergies across these staff functions show promise of greater potential in shared visions, bundled value propositions and cost savings," according to the *Flex Work* authors. However, "organizational capacity must be realigned in order to foster an employee-centered work/life experience."[7]

Five Stages

The Barkley, Cavanaugh, and Miciunas white paper offers a framework to help companies build a highly integrated shared services organization and presents a collaborative model that can be used to assess organizational maturity for supporting a flexible work program in an integrated manner.

As such, the following five stages of flexible working integration are laid out as follows:[7]

Ad hoc. The enterprise does not distinctly recognize or formally support flex work, and singular, individual initiatives are the norm. Prescribed space standards are assigned on the conventional basis of one person per seat.

Experimental. The company recognizes flex work as an effective cost-reduction initiative at a department level, so individual flex work pilots are encouraged by forward-thinking department heads. Mobile and laptop devices are supplied, and variations from traditional space standards are allowed as space-sharing ratios beyond one person per seat are introduced.

Selectively deployed. The potential of flex work to support both departmental and organizational objectives is acknowledged. Strategies are identified and funded as projects at the divisional level across departments.

Formalized. The enterprise recognizes inherent synergies of flex work practices as beneficial to all parties. All divisions and departments take responsibility to proactively incorporate this practice with budget-sharing resources at their fingertips. Training in flex work practices is offered to managers and employees. Furthermore, performance metrics create incentives for space sharing, and participation determines space assignment.

Institutionalized. Flex work becomes a core business strategy, and the "triple bottom line" (e.g., People, Planet and Profit) is embedded into the organizational culture. Enterprise-level support is established, including formal goals, assigned support resources, and formal funding of programs. Aggressive sharing ratios accommodate growth without space expansion. Portfolio footprint is reduced significantly.

Joint Objectives and Unified Metrics

When building an integrated structure on the path toward establishing a highly integrated shared services organization, aligning business performance metrics is key. While consistency in processes and standards across the company might intuitively seem more important, the joint metrics create the all-important accountability.

One common pitfall for companies is that they tend to focus too much on finance metrics, which are easier to measure, and not enough on the human side of the equation, such as understanding attrition rates and why people choose to the leave the company, states Peter Andrew, in a 2014 *The Leader* article, "Let's Stop Talking About the Work Place: Let's Start Talking About the Work Experience."[8]

Ultimately, the Corporate Real Estate 2020 report states that common objectives and unified metrics will work best for companies with a central support function culture for attracting and retaining employees, reinforcing workforce productivity, and enhancing business unit efficiency. This will also help organizations justify investments in revised business and operational processes and increased customer service models.[2]

Missed Opportunities

One common shortcoming in most organizations is that different business units are frequently not on the same page and therefore miss out on many opportunities to optimally support programs and initiatives. Enhancing communication between these business units to establish priorities and align them to business objectives will result in a successful, highly integrated shared services organization.

For example, if a company's real estate and finance groups are not working closely together, then capital budgets might be pushed through without consideration for real estate plans, or real estate decisions might be made without a full appreciation for their funding implications. "This may result in a shortage of or inability to obtain required capital, delays in implementing projects and funding surprises because the capital plan was incomplete," states Steve Silen, KPMG advisory services director, in the white paper, *Real Estate Strategy Alignment: Getting It Right.*[9]

Similarly, if the real estate group is not consulted before a particular business unit makes plans to relocate, renew a lease, or renovate, poor decisions can be made and facilities management may not be equipped to best support employees in their new space. Synergies also need to be present between tax, treasury, and legal departments, particularly for public companies where real estate decisions can impact the tax structure of the company.

A Seat at the Table

Ideally, real estate strategy should be built into a business unit's current and future needs, but this can only be accomplished when the corporate real estate group is provided with adequate information about a department's plans and strategies. Having a seat at the business unit's leadership table is one approach to making sure this information is provided, but more common practices include regular meetings between the real estate and facility management group and the business unit (BU).

Collaborative leadership roundtables where goals are shared and priorities are aligned would be mutually beneficial.

"In essence, the real estate and facility management group needs to be viewed as the BUs' 'trusted advisor,' not an after the fact order taker," explains Silen.[9] In such an arrangement, the real estate group can properly be involved in decisions to acquire, keep, or dispose of properties based on a proper assessment of building conditions and an understanding of operational and maintenance costs.

Bringing IT onto the team will then enable real estate and facility management to most effectively build out the workplace with the right technologies. In other words, establishing joint objectives will provide IT with sufficient time to evaluate technology solutions, obtain funding, and properly install the equipment.

"In addition, the real estate and facility management team needs to understand the IT impacts before acquiring or disposing of real estate space, and the costs of relocating data centers or installing/removing IT equipment must be factored into the real estate strategy," Silen points out.[9]

Aligning planning with procurement offers the opportunity to achieve corporate financial goals as well as protect the corporate brand. A key strategy for procurement organizations is to provide a strong core team that ensures process, tools, skills, relationships, and metrics are in place to enable the business teams to manage suppliers effectively.

Yet another example is aligning the real estate and facility management team with human resources. Because it often manages amenities such as cafés, fitness centers, and on-site day care, it is essential for real estate and facility management to understand HR's plans and strategies for these services so space can be sufficiently allocated and built out.

Conclusion

High-performance corporations are demanding ever-greater efficiencies of their infrastructure and support services in order to remain competitive. This requires deeper forms of collaboration among corporate real estate, HR, IT and other enterprise support functions.

Corporate real estate leaders have an opportunity to begin facilitating conversations with their peer organizations about the value and importance of closer collaboration and partnering. Collaborating on major projects, such as a new office or a major workplace transformation, can be a productive place to start.

This can lay the groundwork and help build relationships for ongoing partnering at a higher, more strategic level, and can help elevate corporate real estate's value and overall contribution to the success of the corporation.

Giving some additional food for thought, CBRE's Andrew offers the following: "To leverage the true value of the partnership between the various enterprise support functions, focus needs to shift from the work place to the work experience. It is through this shift that the support functions can be enablers of enterprise transformation and business improvement."[8]

References

1. Boulanger, P. (2012). *Trends in shared services: Unlocking the full potential.* Report from eleventh annual Accenture Global Shared Services Conference. Retrieved from http://www.cas-ag.eu/SiteCollectionDocuments/PDF/Accenture-Unlocking-Full-Potential-Shared-Services-Presentation-Script.pdf

2. CoreNet Global. (2012, May). *Corporate real estate 2020: Partnering with key support functions.* Retrieved from https://resources.corenetglobal.org/knowledgecenteronline/SearchByTopicAndResource.aspx?ID=4754

3. Murphy, K. (1998). *Procurement partnering.* Retrieved from http://www.landandmaritime.dla.mil/downloads/legal/adr/dlapubs/Partnering.pdf

4. Andrew, P., Mackenzie, I., & Fanoe, M. (2012). *Partnering with key support functions.* Presentation made at CoreNet Global Singapore Summit, 2012.

5. Partnering with key support functions: The importance of integrated resource modeling. (2012, September/October). *The Leader.* Available from https://resources.corenetglobal.org/knowledgecenteronline/SearchByTopicAndResource.aspx

6. Kamath, N., & Horton, I. (2012, November/December). "Upskilling" the organization advances relationship building, cross-functional collaboration and change management. *The Leader.* Retrieved from https://resources.corenetglobal.org/knowledgecenteronline/SearchByTopicAndResource.aspx

7. Barkley, L., Cavanaugh, K., & Miciunas, G. (2012, June). *Flex work: A collaborative model for FM, HR & IT.* Retrieved from https://resources.corenetglobal.org/knowledgecenteronline/SearchByTopicAndResource.aspx?ID=816

8. Andrew, P. (2014, May/June). Let's stop talking about the work place: Let's start talking about the work experience. *The Leader.* Retrieved from http://theleader.epubxp.com/i/303516-may-jun-2014/15

9. Silen, S. (2012, May). *Real estate strategy alignment: Getting it right.* KPMG International Shared Services and Outsourcing Advisory. Retrieved from https://resources.corenetglobal.org/knowledgecenteronline/SearchByTopicAndResource.aspx?ID=4416

Chapter 16

Enterprise Leadership

Summary

Years ago, senior corporate real estate executives could be considered successful leaders if they simply delivered projects ahead of schedule and under budget. While these abilities are still valued, much more is required today, when both the demands upon and the opportunities before corporate real estate are significantly greater.

In 2012, CoreNet Global delivered its Corporate Real Estate 2020 research initiative, which explored the future of the corporate real estate profession across eight dimensions, including leadership. The research found that in order to be a true enterprise leader – one who creates and deploys corporate real estate strategies as part of overall business strategy – the corporate real estate executive of the future needs to evolve from a subject-matter specialist in real estate to a strategic partner with a broad knowledge of the business. This would effectively position corporate real estate as not just a support function or an "order-taker," but as a strategic advisor and an "equal partner to and for the business."[1]

This chapter examines the concept of enterprise leadership and illustrates how corporate real estate leaders can best leverage the real estate portfolio to drive greater corporate performance. Enterprise leadership is defined in section one; section two examines enterprise leadership in the context of corporate real estate responsibilities and its expansion beyond traditional corporate real estate functions. Section three offers predictions, observations, and findings on enterprise leadership from the CoreNet Global Corporate Real Estate 2020 research initiative.

What Is Enterprise Leadership?

Simply put, an enterprise leadership approach puts the success of the enterprise first and foremost above all other considerations. This management style employs a centralized, integrated approach, and leaders are charged with building connections across—not just within—multiple business units, functions, and / or locations. An enterprise perspective, as opposed to a business unit perspective, develops and leverages synergies and efficiencies to deliver benefits that no single entity of the business would be capable of capturing on its own.

From a corporate real estate management perspective, enterprise leadership also means not viewing real estate as an end unto itself, but rather as an enabler to the success of the corporation – to the overall enterprise. It requires that senior corporate real estate executives think and act like more like senior business executives. Consider this viewpoint from Mike Napier, Chief Executive for Real Estate, Shell International, when he was interviewed for *The Leader* in 2004:

> "We're trying to change everybody's approach within Shell Real Estate Services to think of themselves as a business professional first, and a real estate professional second, rather than the other way around. I think this is quite significant. Because if we continue to sit on our side of the fence, on our side of the relationship, as merely real estate professionals without really understanding what the business issues and drivers are, we'll always be viewed as a service provider only. And as such, somebody will challenge us on what value we add above and beyond the market. Our value has to be our intimate knowledge of Shell, our intimate knowledge of how the business runs and what the business drivers are."[2]

Sarah Abrams, Senior Vice President and Head of Global Real Estate at Iron Mountain, offered a similar perspective as part of the Corporate Real Estate 2020 research:

> "Figuring out the best way to integrate real estate as an enabler to the business requires you to really understand the business. Effective corporate real estate leaders must also

be very good, polished sales and relationship people. They need to be able to sell the vision and the value proposition of real estate as a business enabler."[1]

From Corporate Decentralization to Global Alignment

The current emphasis on enterprise leadership marks a distinct change from the 1980s and early 1990s, when corporate decentralization resulted in a focus on developing strong leadership silos at the business unit level. Successful leaders of this era were often seen as unquestioned drivers of their singular unit's products and services and were rewarded for individual gains.[3]

However, in the early 2000s, corporations entered an era of increased global competition, cost pressures, and disruptive technologies, among other challenges. To deal with these complexities, leading organizations began aligning and integrating operations and efforts in the name of enterprise performance.

Douglas A. Ready, Senior Lecturer in Organizational Effectiveness at the MIT Sloan School of Management, has suggested four responsibilities incumbent upon all enterprise leaders:

1. They must focus organizational attention on the customer and prevent distractions from that goal.

2. They must assist the entire organization in building the capabilities required for working together toward effective enterprise leadership.

3. They must be able to reconcile the tensions that exist in any organization that could impede progress toward the larger business goal.

4. They must create alignment "by building consistency between an organization's statements of purpose, its processes, and the skills and behaviors required of its people."[3]

Expanding Role of Corporate Real Estate in the Enterprise

Within the corporate real estate profession, a parallel evolution has occurred as many corporations have adopted centralized organizational models, in turn maximizing their potential enterprise-wide impact. In some corporations, corporate real estate is organized within a broader shared services group, which can further boost performance through greater collaboration and synergy.

Corporate real estate organizations acquire knowledge of current and projected business activities through ongoing client relationship management activities that align the real estate portfolio with future business needs. In addition, collaborating and partnering more closely with other key support functions, such as IT and HR, have given corporate real estate new opportunities to contribute at an enterprise level.

Corporate real estate executives also can play an important role in creating an enterprise-wide location strategy for offices, data centers, R&D operations, production and logistics facilities that enables access to talent, markets, and supply-chain advantages while minimizing costs and operational risks.

Refocusing Beyond Business Units

Faced with the day-to-day demands of transactions, projects, and facility management, corporate real estate professionals can find it challenging to look beyond short-term, unit-specific needs in order to optimize long-term enterprise initiatives. One solution is to analyze corporate real estate decisions through one of three possible approaches: business optimal, real estate optimal, or enterprise optimal.

Business optimal strategies provide maximized steps to goals from a specific—and often single—business unit. Real estate optimal strategies typically optimize the real estate portfolio's perceived performance through a combination of lower costs, reduced vacancies, and minimized real estate risks. Enterprise optimal strategies address the net impacts on other business units, as well as impacts on market presence, political commitments, talent and labor pools, and finance.[4]

A decision to employ the first two strategies will often produce short-term wins under the initial project analysis, yet it will also present a new and long-term need to reevaluate decisions as the enterprise evolution continues and data-driven analysis expands around nonintegrated performance outliers that neither support nor fit within a modern, agile, and flexible business structure.

New Skill Sets Required

The Corporate Real Estate 2020 Enterprise Leadership final report recommended that senior leaders develop certain skills to function as true enterprise leaders. Participants underscored the need for a broad, functional awareness of business that incorporates a working knowledge of IT, HR, and finance disciplines and the ability to foster collaborative relationships with these functions to help their companies pursue greater efficiencies through economies of scale.[5]

The report further suggested that mastery of "the basics" of corporate real estate will become an assumed skill in the future:

> "Today's senior leaders are moving beyond the targeting of operational efficiencies and cost reduction measures as they identify areas to add enterprise value in fields like employee retention and engagement, enhancing collaboration and innovation, and conveying the culture and brand to the employees and customers working and visiting the space. To effect this evolution, these leaders must demonstrate the requisite business management skills to integrate real estate as an enabler in the business, and they must be able to communicate in the language of the business."[5]

Successful enterprise leaders also need highly refined "soft skills" capabilities. Senior corporate real estate professionals will be expected to identify, explain, promote, and ultimately build consensus toward the changes they are driving. To do so, they must become highly competent change management leaders.

In a 2011 Johnson Controls/CoreNet Global survey of corporate real estate professionals, respondents stated that change management is one of the most important components of the enterprise leader skill set (along with relationship management, strategic thinking, and cross-functional collaborations). Asked to break down time they spent managing change, survey respondents reported that as much as 50% is spent communicating with employees and stakeholders to manage actual and potential resistance to change, 25% is spent on technical issues like project planning or data gathering, and 25% is spent on financial issues such as mapping return on investment and initiative funding. Survey respondents gave themselves very mixed reviews on their change management capabilities.[6]

A 2011 CBRE/CoreNet Global survey confirmed that "soft" business skills are seen as increasingly important—relationship building, strategic thinking, cross-functional collaboration, and change management. However, more than half of those who rate strategic thinking and change management as high in importance also report gaps in those skills within their own teams.[7] In order to bridge the "soft skills" gap, 10% of participants in the survey said they plan to use service providers and consultants to obtain the needed expertise. Significantly, 72% plan to train existing staff, and 10% will hire new staff to bridge the skills gap.

The Future of Enterprise Leadership and Corporate Real Estate

As part of the Corporate Real Estate 2020 research process, the member-led enterprise leadership research team created a series of "bold statements" or predictions about the state of enterprise leadership (e.g., in the context of corporate real estate management) in the year 2020. Those predictions included:[1]

- By 2020, senior leaders will evolve from subject matter specialists focused on execution to integrators, change agents and strategists who are viewed internally as an essential, equal partner to and for the business.

- Senior leaders will be competent in the core business and possess a skill set that is diversified, cross-functional and focused on customer relationship and process management. They will advocate sustainability and corporate social responsibility goals.

- Senior leaders will champion the integration of leading-edge technology into real estate/workplace operations and into the workplace itself to support increased employee productivity and an enhanced employee experience.

- Senior leaders will be able to measure the impact of workplace infrastructure on business units and the enterprise.

- Senior leaders will champion change in the supply side of the service industry, including more innovative partnerships and the seamless integration of internal and external resources globally.

- In support of a global, mobile work force, senior leaders will lead the development of improved corporate solutions that elevate the brand, promote the culture and assure employee engagement, particularly for client-facing space.

Conclusion

To become true enterprise leaders, increase their value to their companies and help secure a seat at the table with senior management, the CoreNet Global 2020 report on enterprise leadership suggests that corporate real estate professionals:[1]

- Develop a broad-based, functional awareness of their business, to include a working knowledge of IT, HR and finance disciplines.

- Demonstrate the requisite business management skills to leverage real estate as an enabler in the business and further develop sales skills to influence across the organization.

- Evolve beyond the transactional to the strategic level to think like a shareholder and approach situations from a business perspective as opposed to a strictly real estate perspective.

- Embrace and foster collaborative relationships with IT and HR as companies pursue greater efficiencies through economies of scale.

- Master the basics of corporate real estate to evolve beyond targeting operational efficiencies and overall cost reduction measures to identify opportunities for business expansion by articulating clear visions and clearly translating business strategies into organizational change.

• Centralize the corporate real estate function to operate across regions or business lines as appropriate to include overall transaction management, workplace planning, overall portfolio strategy, general governance and oversight.

References

1. CoreNet Global. (2012, May). Corporate Real Estate 2020 Final Report: Enterprise Leadership. Retrieved from https://resources.corenetglobal.org/knowledgecenteronline/SearchByTopicAndResource.aspx?ID=532

2. CoreNet Global. (2004, September/October). Shell International's Mike Napier: "We're Business People First, Real Estate People Second." *The Leader.* Retrieved from https://resources.corenetglobal.org/knowledgecenteronline/SearchByTopicAndResource.aspx?ID=61

3. Ready, D. A. (2004, Spring). Leading at the enterprise level. *MIT Sloan Management Review.*

4. Berthold, B. (2014, August). Enterprise alignment: What do you align with? [PowerPoint presentation]. Master of Corporate Real Estate Class, Irvine, CA. Retrieved from http://www.corenetglobal.org/files/summits_events/LasVegas2013/images/3-EA_What_do_you_align_with_2012.pdf

5. CoreNet Global. (2012, September/October). Enterprise leadership: The collaborative, value-adding role of the future. *The Leader.* Retrieved from https://resources.corenetglobal.org/knowledgecenteronline/SearchByTopicAndResource.aspx?ID=568

6. Bohn, J., Hughes, J. D., & Tare, S. (2011). *Change management needs a change lead and human touch.* Johnson Controls, CoreNet Global. Retrieved from http://www.corenetglobal.org/files/global/pdf/Johnson%20Controls_ChangeMgmt_WebinarPresentation_final%20(3).pdf

7. Kamath, N., & Horton, I. (2012, November/December). "Upskilling" the organization advances relationship building, cross-functional collaboration and change management. *The Leader.* Retrieved from https://resources.corenetglobal.org/knowledgecenteronline/SearchByTopicAndResource.aspx?ID=1668

Chapter 17

The Future of Corporate Real Estate

Summary

Companies are changing the way they do business in response to globalization, influences that transform the workplace into workspace, and a constantly shifting environment of macroeconomic forces. In fast-moving companies seeking competitive advantage, these forces are prompting corporate real estate professionals to take on new roles, moving from a transaction-based cost center to a strategic asset that manages functions adding value to the enterprises. This chapter delves into these trends, and their likely continuing impact on corporate real estate far into the future.

The chapter is divided into four sections. Woven throughout are the findings from the year-long research project by CoreNet Global, Corporate Real Estate 2020. In that project, hundreds of corporate real estate leaders worldwide provided predictions and insights into the profession's future. Eight senior leader research groups made predictions about corporate real estate spanning enterprise leadership, location strategy, and the role of place, how corporate real estate will partner with key support functions, portfolio optimization and asset management, service delivery and outsourcing, sustainability, and technology tools.

The eight Corporate Real Estate 2020 research reports and the future trends they identified have stimulated additional research and information on the transformative period that business enterprises and corporate real estate are experiencing. Some of these examinations are also included here.

In section one of this chapter, "The Emerging Business Model," current and future influences of new technologies, global change, workplace, sustainability, and other drivers are explored, along with the new business model's evolving impact on corporate real estate. Section two summarizes some key predictions about the ongoing transformation of corporate real estate from research reports in Corporate Real Estate 2020 and other sources. Section three considers some new skills corporate real estate executives will need to prepare for these roles.

The Emerging Business Model

Companies are being compelled to completely rethink their business models in order to remain competitive. The new model is responding to forces including rapid technology changes, evolving workspace needs, globalization and its accompanying cultural forces, the increasing importance of sustainability, and the need for fluid real estate in a highly complex business environment set against a backdrop of economic uncertainties in both developing and mature markets.

Technology Drivers

The most powerful forces in the emerging business model have been technology advances. Consumer-oriented technology products have greatly contributed to transforming the workplace, so that now much work gets done through BYOD (bring your own device), mobile device management (MDM), mobile application management (MAM), desktop and app virtualization, file sharing and sync, web-based remote support and collaboration, and enterprise app store solutions.[1]

Companies are reporting that workplace mobility programs generate bottom-line savings of as much as 30%. These changes are evolving "workplace" into "work presence" and spurring a rethinking of how work takes place in companies' physical space. Collaboration hubs and drop-in offices are replacing meeting rooms and traditional offices.

Cisco estimates that, by 2020, 50 billion devices and objects will be connected to the internet, collecting data, reporting efficiency and indicating performance factors[2]. Corporate real estate has begun managing significant portions of data capture and analysis, planning the spaces where equipment resides, evaluating what security is required, and determining how this affects personnel needs. Concurrently, much of this data helps corporate real estate measure its own impact on the bottom line and make visible its strategic importance for the enterprise.3 While it holds promise for better needs forecasting and other business function analytics, there are also problems with how best to pull and evaluate streams of data from multiple sources across many platforms.

Nonetheless, more companies will rush to implement the training and processes needed to capture and analyze big data for competitive advantage. Corporations are planning data centers to accommodate these needs. The sophistication and capabilities for data collection and analysis will continue to improve in order to achieve the most efficient utilization.

People-Centric Enterprise

The development of social networks and other customer-oriented technologies are moving the customer from passive recipient to co-collaborator—impacting brands, products, and corporate reputation. As consumers become the primary drivers of product and service design in many businesses, reaching them through social networks has become integral to marketing products and maintaining exceptional customer relations.

At the same time, the industrial era mentality of employees as a cog in the enterprise is changing to one that has people at the center.[4] The multigenerational workforce and continued globalization are requiring deeper analysis of workers' varying needs—for their satisfaction and productivity purposes and so that the company can attract the best and brightest. Collaborative workspaces and work from anywhere are becoming major business model influences as organizations reacts to this work style's competitive advantage, lower per employee costs, and popularity with employees.

Corporate Real Estate's Transformation

As corporations respond to the macro forces prompting business model changes, the face of corporate real estate will also change. As workplaces change, corporate real estate increasingly finds itself in the driver's seat as support services work together to put customers, employees, and service providers at the center of the enterprise value equation.

In high-performing companies, corporate real estate has already begun to take advantage of its position in the center of workspace, talent recruitment, employee satisfaction, and corporate branding. It is assuming an enterprise leader role in the arena of what is being called "work-life supports," ensuring optimal work experience and enhanced employee productivity.

Portfolio Optimization

Participants in the Corporate Real Estate 2020 research saw the enterprise portfolio concept evolving from its traditional focus on real property and fixed assets to a broader view that includes "human and capital resources, technology and other components that contribute to a company's ability to compete in a global marketplace" (Pierce, p. 8).[5] As globalization has opened up new markets for products and services, companies have to deal with an increasing number of market and regulatory forces.

Advances in technology will enable more accurate and timely collection of the data needed for effective analysis of portfolio assets, but the complexity of managing this data may increase as new types of tools become integrated into the enterprise. While improvements in demand forecasting are anticipated by some senior leaders, others are skeptical of this outcome due to the complexity of variables involved.[5]

The variables that make up location analysis continue to grow more complex. The uncertainties of external factors will drive corporate real estate professionals to provide built-in flexibility to respond to external exigencies.

Current considerations include sustainability, unpredictable oil prices, ongoing cost containment pressures, rebound in corporate growth, flexible work strategies, and the need to weigh developing country benefits against potential economic and political instability. For example, more than one third of 150 senior finance executives in major corporations surveyed in a 2014 IBM report expected their North American assets to increase over the next three years. About one third saw similar plans for Mexico and China.[6] Many of these considerations are likely to remain in place until 2024.

Corporate Real Estate 2020 research participants expected global labor shortages in the skilled trades to remain a factor, especially in multinational corporations.[7] The current recovery in domestic manufacturing is also expected to continue into 2020 in most developed countries due to the decline of cost advantages that led offshoring. Offshore labor costs have risen, and sustainability has come into play as an influence.

Corporate Real Estate 2020 participants believed that simplifying the supply chain will present an important business advantage. Having large, stable markets nearby, shorter product delivery times, lower inventory carrying costs, higher manufacturing quality, and presence of nearby outsourcers are all factors that are becoming more important in location cost benefit analyses. These elements have already spurred the reshoring of manufacturing. Supply chain management will be expected to cut costs and duplication wherever possible, exploring new ways to impact performance.[8]

Discussing the future of supply chain management and site selection at a CoreNet Global Summit in 2014, Renee Buck, of international consulting firm Buck Consultants, echoed the expectation that supply chain management will move up the list of business priorities. He foresees a supply chain with greater flexibility to increase responsiveness to rapidly changing markets and a shift from mass markets to niche markets, with supply chain becoming part of the core business.[9]

Integrated Support Services

The need for IT, HR, finance, and corporate real estate to move beyond their core roles and collaborate on enterprise-wide strategies has been discussed extensively in recent years. Systematic research surveys by global management consulting firms like Accenture and Deloitte were among the first to point out the need for such collaboration, and they began capturing the annual progress toward these goals.

The development of such a collaborative support group model would bring together the legacy support functions and serve as a resource to enable a more satisfactory work experience, higher productivity and lower costs. While continuing to deliver support to the business units, "strategy, including internal business unit relationship management, planning and innovation will be elevated and integrated within this new support group entity," (*Executive Summary*, p. 8).[8]

This model would require a gradual process to implement, perhaps beginning with focused project collaborations, and should be customized to the needs of the enterprise. Corporate Real Estate 2020 research pointed out that corporate real estate's position in the enterprise naturally lends itself to becoming the driver of "super nucleus" team collaboration. Over 60% of the senior leaders in the 2020 research project agreed with the super nucleus predictions.[10]

The global shared services model was adopted early by leading corporations such as Procter & Gamble. As the cost and revenue benefits continue to grow, it is anticipated that more global corporations will move into this expansive approach.

Outsourcing

From its evolution in the 1990s, when the economic recession drove large occupiers to seek greater efficiencies and corporate real estate became a go-to source for cost savings and outsourcing, multiple outsourcing models have come into play. They range from the early service provider and preferred provider models to exclusive provider, outsourced partner, and collaborative or strategic alliance relationships to meet the varying needs of major corporation customers. Much like the corporations they serve, service providers are shifting from cost-based thinking to the broader definition of "value" their clients must address.

"In the 2000s, globalization, information technology, administrative organizational structure and labor combined with economic fluctuation to reshape and redefine internal and external real estate service delivery. ... Corporations began integrating and leveraging external providers for strategic corporate real estate service delivery" (Pierce, p. 17).[5]

Service providers may be engaged to help with strategic global portfolio optimization, workplace mobility, process improvement, energy management, and sustainability.

Corporate Real Estate 2020's service delivery and outsourcing research teams predicted that service providers will more routinely be expected to go beyond the task-oriented work of transactions and asked to manage services provided by other vendors, even to consult with the corporation on its strategic vision.[11] Some will provide a comprehensive set of bundled services and take on more risk and reward in their partnerships. This predicted move is already occurring in many corporations. As internal company resources become increasingly focused on their strategic roles, service providers will play an important part in effecting the collaborative support group model.

New Corporate Real Estate Skill Sets

Enterprise Leadership

New management skills will be required as the corporate real estate function evolves in many corporations from a narrow set of operational responsibilities to a broader strategic asset with input on branding, employee recruitment, productivity, and more. Corporate real estate leaders will take on the mantle of enterprise leadership when they gain a full understanding of the "business of the business," learn to "speak the language" of the C-suite, and take up the challenge to contribute enterprise-wide value. They should be able to identify opportunities, synergies, risks, and efficiencies across multiple facets of the enterprise.

Change Management

Enterprise leaders must become highly competent change management leaders. They will be expected to identify, explain, promote, and ultimately build consensus toward the changes they are driving for the enterprise. A 2011 Johnson Controls/CoreNet Global survey revealed that relationship management, strategic thinking, cross-functional collaboration, change management, and influencing are considered to be the most important components of the enterprise leader skill set.

A 2011 CBRE/CoreNet Global survey also confirmed that "soft" business skills—relationship building, strategic thinking, cross-functional collaboration, and change management—are seen as increasingly important (see Figure 17.1). However, corporate real estate leaders are reporting capability gaps in these skills. More than half of those who rate strategic thinking and change management as high in importance also report gaps in those skills within their own team.[12]

With corporate real estate professionals rating themselves poorly on their change management capabilities and other increasingly important "soft skills," this will be a critical area for professional development. Most of the corporate real estate executives surveyed in the 2011 CBRE/CoreNet Global survey report plans to train their staff in these areas.

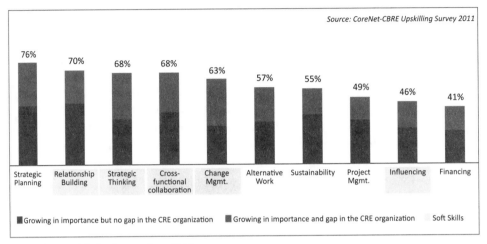

Figure 17.1. Assessing Skills

Big Data Skills

A strong analytic skill set will be needed by corporate real estate professionals, not only to capture big data in ways that can be readily accessed, but also so they can decide what data is important and how various data streams can be best cross-referenced to create compelling business cases. This critical competency is needed so that organizations can translate what the business is doing back into corporate real estate decisions.

Sustainability

As sustainability has progressed from a marginal consideration to a more mainstream one, it has impacted the business bottom line, employee well-being, corporate branding, and corporate public relations. These concerns have several intersection points with corporate real estate, from workplace branding to employee recruitment to customer satisfaction. Corporate real estate executives in the future will be expected to understand sustainability issues and how they can potentially impact the enterprise.

As sustainability issues continue to gain traction, corporate real estate will be making the business case for it and promoting and tracking it across the corporation. Predictions include the likelihood that real estate portfolios will be restructured, buildings interconnected on microgrids, and advances in energy storage put in place in ways that impact "building operations, transportation and planning" (*Executive Summary*, p, 20).[8] Environmental impact measurements will also be implemented and linked to enterprise-wide data to track results. Corporate Real Estate 2020 research participants also predicted an increase in sustainability regulations by 2020 to ensure the efficient use of resources by corporations, along with penalties for noncompliance.

As the future corporate real estate professionals help drive changes to ensure sustainable operations, they will work with sustainability experts to see that the change implemented meets corporate sustainability goals. Corporations are approaching this envisioned future at different rates of speed driven by their geographic reach, size, culture, worker needs, and other factors.[8]

Corporate Branding

A strong corporate brand adds significant value to the corporation. Not only does it enhance customer outreach and engagement, it aids in employee recruitment and public relations with local and global communities. Corporate real estate can add value to the brand through real estate assets including building design, building selection, naming, and workspace design. Corporate real estate's involvement in site location strategies, workplace, and workspace will make understanding branding an increasingly important knowledge set for corporate real estate executives.

Conclusion

Corporate real estate is on a journey of evolution. It is evolving from a cost-focused, execution-oriented support function to a value-adding strategic asset that can help the corporation achieve its goals. This is the future of corporate real estate.

Different companies are at different points along that evolutionary path. As a result, it is essential for corporate real estate professionals to become "students of the business," understand the key drivers for corporate success and ensure alignment between real estate and the enterprises they serve.

Irrespective of industry sector, corporate real estate professionals often report that agility, innovation, cost containment, globalization, sustainability, risk mitigation, and employee retention and satisfaction are priorities for their companies' senior management. Each of these drivers or priorities represents an opportunity for corporate real estate to align, lead, demonstrate value and achieve its full potential. For corporate real estate professionals who are prepared to seize these opportunities, the future is bright.

References

1. Citrix Systems, & Bourne, V. (2013). *Mobility in business report.* Ft. Lauderdale, FL: Citrix Systems.

2. Freshfields Bruckhaus Deringer. (2015). Retrieved from www.freshfields.com/en/global/Digital/Internet_of_things

3. Ferguson Partners. (2014). *Moving at the speed of business: Data may be the ultimate answer as corporate real estate strives for relevancy.* Chicago, IL.

4. Govaars, S. (2011, January). *Five forces and the next era in corporate real estate.* CoreNet Global Industry Tracker/Member ViewPoint. Atlanta, GA: CoreNet.

5. Pierce, K. (2012). *Corporate real estate 2020 final report: Portfolio optimization and asset management.* Atlanta, GA: CoreNet Global.

6. Mattson-Teig, B. (2015, January/February). View from the C-Suite. *The Leader.* Retrieved from http://theleader.epubxp.com/i/436073-jan-feb-2015/22

7. CoreNet Global. (2012, September/October). Enterprise leadership: The collaborative, value-adding role of the future. *The Leader.* Retrieved from https://resources.corenet-global.org/knowledgecenteronline/SearchByTopicAndResource.aspx?ID=568

8. Kadzis, R. (2012, May). *Corporate real estate 2020 final report: Executive summary.* Atlanta, GA: CoreNet Global.

9. Buck, R. (2014, September). Changing supply chains impact effective site selections. Presentation made at CoreNet Global Summit, Berlin, Germany.

10. Robinson, C., & Colman, C. (2013). *Making the case for the super nucleus.* Retrieved from http://info.cassidyturley.com/blog/bid/320892/Making-the-Case-for-the-Super-Nucleus

11. Brister, K., Layda, B., & Ochalla, K. (2012, May). *Corporate real estate 2020 final report: Service delivery and outsourcing.* Atlanta, GA: CoreNet Global.

12. Kamath, N., & Horton, I. (2015, November/December). "Upskilling" the organization advances relationship building, cross-functional collaboration and change management. *The Leader.* Available from https://resources.corenetglobal.org/knowledgecenteronline/SearchByTopicAndResource.aspx?ID=1668

Appendix

Suggested Reading

Readers interested in learning more on the topics associated with the chapters within this book are encouraged to review the resources listed below.

Chapter 1

Apgar, Mahlon, IV. (2009, Nov. 30). What every leader should know about real estate. The Economist Intelligence Unit in partnership with Harvard Business School Publishing. *Harvard Business Review.* https://resources.corenetglobal.org/knowledgecenteronline/SearchByTopicAndResource.aspx?ID=4143

Chotipanich, S. (2004). Positioning facility management. *Facilities, 22*(13/14), 364–372.

CoreNet Global & CBRE. *"Upskilling" the corporate real estate organization: Survey results.* https://resources.corenetglobal.org/knowledgecenteronline/SearchByTopicAndResource.aspx?ID=2498

CoreNet Global. *2012 CoreNet Global state of the industry.* https://resources.corenetglobal.org/knowledgecenteronline/SearchByTopicAndResource.aspx?ID=2833

CoreNet Global. *Corporate Real Estate 2020 final report: Executive summary.* https://resources.corenetglobal.org/knowledgecenteronline/SearchByTopicAndResource.aspx?ID=3981

CoreNet Global. *The importance of corporate real estate management in overall corporate strategies.* https://resources.corenetglobal.org/knowledgecenteronline/SearchByTopicAndResource.aspx?ID=3517

CoreNet Global. *Leading the corporate real estate enterprise: Perspectives from Plato, Aristotle and Milton Friedman.* https://resources.corenetglobal.org/knowledgecenteronline/SearchByTopicAndResource.aspx?ID=4511

CoreNet Global. *Real estate professionals vs. business professional? Corporate real estate's role in influencing business strategy.* https://resources.corenetglobal.org/knowledgecenteronline/SearchByTopicAndResource.aspx?ID=1926

CoreNet Global. *The relevance of corporate real estate to enterprise success.* https://resources.corenetglobal.org/knowledgecenteronline/SearchByTopicAndResource.aspx?ID=5694

CoreNet Global. *Unilever's Agile Program.* https://resources.corenetglobal.org/knowledgecenteronline/SearchByTopicAndResource.aspx?ID=2581

Varcoe, B. (2000). Implications for facility management of the changing business climate. *Facilities, 18*(10/11/12), 383–391.

Chapter 2

Blue Point Strategies. (2014). *Retail site selection checklist.* http://www.bluepointstrategies.com/uploads/Retail_Site_Selection_Checklist.pdf

Booth, T. (2013, January 9). Here, there, and everywhere (global shoring). *The Economist.* http://www.economist.com/news/special-report/21569572-after-decades-sending-work-across-world-companies-are-rethinking-their-offshoring

Colliers. *European Industrial and Logistics: A Long-Term View.* https://resources.corenetglobal.org/knowledgecenteronline/SearchByTopicAndResource.aspx?ID=5715

CoreNet Global. *Breakout session 8: Corporate real estate 2020 location strategy and the role of place.* https://resources.corenetglobal.org/knowledgecenteronline/SearchByTopicAndResource.aspx?ID=551

CoreNet Global. *CoreNet Global location strategy survey 2012: Leading practices related to effective location strategy.* https://resources.corenetglobal.org/knowledgecenteronline/SearchByTopicAndResource.aspx?ID=2498?ID=3038

CoreNet Global. *The future of globalization.* https://resources.corenetglobal.org/knowledgecenteronline/SearchByTopicAndResource.aspx?ID=1532

CoreNet Global. *Location strategy and the role of place: Manufacturing moves west, and the war for talent and space will still reign.* https://resources.corenetglobal.org/knowledgecenteronline/SearchByTopicAndResource.aspx?ID=731

CoreNet Global. *Secret weapons: How corporate real estate executives are researching the best expansion locations.* https://resources.corenetglobal.org/knowledgecenteronline/SearchByTopicAndResource.aspx?ID=2454

CoreNet Global. *Perspectives on location strategy.* https://resources.corenetglobal.org/knowledgecenteronline/SearchByTopicAndResource.aspx?ID=1383

CoreNet Global. *Using effective location and metro planning to influence business strategy.* https://resources.corenetglobal.org/knowledgecenteronline/SearchByTopicAndResource.aspx?ID=3297

Gartner Supply Chain Top 25 for 2014. http://www.gartner.com/technology/supply-chain/top25.jsp

Jones Lang LaSalle. *Re-engineering the cost structure of the business footprint.* https://resources.corenetglobal.org/knowledgecenteronline/SearchByTopicAndResource.aspx?ID=3125

Siemens. (2013, March). *Self-organizing factories: Pictures of the future.* http://www.siemens.com/innovation/en/home/pictures-of-the-future/industry-and-automation/digtial-factory-trends-industry-4-0.html

Chapter 3

CoreNet Global. *Corporate real estate 2020 final report: Portfolio optimization and asset management.* https://resources.corenetglobal.org/knowledgecenteronline/SearchByTopicAndResource.aspx?ID=2511

CoreNet Global. *Fact or fiction: Proactive portfolio management.* https://resources.corenetglobal.org/knowledgecenteronline/SearchByTopicAndResource.aspx?ID=2346

CoreNet Global. *Managing and optimising the portfolio: Balancing cost, flexibility and risk.* https://resources.corenetglobal.org/knowledgecenteronline/SearchByTopicAndResource.aspx?ID=1662

CoreNet Global. *Portfolio management from every angle: Development of the first long range plan for a major global portfolio.* https://resources.corenetglobal.org/knowledgecenteronline/SearchByTopicAndResource.aspx?ID=3243

CoreNet Global. *Portfolio optimization and asset management: The definition is evolving to a networked enterprise without geographic boundaries.* https://resources.corenetglobal.org/knowledgecenteronline/SearchByTopicAndResource.aspx?ID=6478

CoreNet Global. *Unlocking the hidden value in your portfolio.* https://resources.corenetglobal.org/knowledgecenteronline/SearchByTopicAndResource.aspx?ID=1584

Newmark Knight Frank. *Portfolio: Drive productivity . . . and reduce cost!* https://resources.corenetglobal.org/knowledgecenteronline/SearchByTopicAndResource.aspx?ID=2060

Unilever. *Portfolio optimization at Unilever.* https://resources.corenetglobal.org/knowledgecenteronline/SearchByTopicAndResource.aspx?ID=3588

Chapter 4

CB Richard Ellis. *Global office development cycle: Where are we now?* https://resources.corenet-global.org/knowledgecenteronline/SearchByTopicAndResource.aspx?ID=5855

Constructing Excellence. (2006, February). *Whole life costing.* http://www.constructingex-cellence.org.uk/resources/themes/business/wholelifecosting.jsp

CoRE Fundamentals. *Lifecycle.* http://corenetglobal.articulate-online.com/ContentRegistration.aspx?DocumentID=37fffe71–5b90–4b3a-9bef-f2228e4e6ccf&Cust=30443&ReturnUrl=/p/3044377392

CoreNet Global. *Facility management and life-cycle design.* https://resources.corenetglobal.org/knowledgecenteronline/SearchByTopicAndResource.aspx?ID=4294

CoreNet Global. *Grave to cradle: Bringing blighted real estate (and communities) back to life.* https://resources.corenetglobal.org/knowledgecenteronline/SearchByTopicAndResource.aspx?ID=4854

CoreNet Global. *Life cycle asset management at Toyota: Doing more with less.* https://resources.corenetglobal.org/knowledgecenteronline/SearchByTopicAndResource.aspx?ID=2343

CoreNet Global. *Proactive asset management: Integrating facilities management with business priorities.* https://resources.corenetglobal.org/knowledgecenteronline/SearchByTopicAndResource.aspx?ID=3745

CoreNet Global. *Taking charge of capital spend and asset management.* https://resources.corenetglobal.org/knowledgecenteronline/SearchByTopicAndResource.aspx?ID=5606

CoreNet Global. *The changing nature of the CRE agenda in the economic cycle.* https://resources.corenetglobal.org/knowledgecenteronline/SearchByTopicAndResource.aspx?ID=5458

CoreNet Global. *The surplus property dilemma: Donation, what a practical solution.* https://resources.corenetglobal.org/knowledgecenteronline/SearchByTopicAndResource.aspx?ID=2562

Fuller, S. *Life cycle cost analysis (LCCA).* http://www.wbdg.org/resources/lcca.php

Chapter 5

CBRE. *Office leasing around the world.* https://resources.corenetglobal.org/knowledgecenteronline/SearchByTopicAndResource.aspx?ID=3050

CoreNet Global. *If you can't be with the lease you love, love the lease you're with.* https://resources.corenetglobal.org/knowledgecenteronline/SearchByTopicAndResource.aspx?ID=4807

CoreNet Global. *M&A and divestiture bulletin.* https://resources.corenetglobal.org/knowledgecenteronline/SearchByTopicAndResource.aspx?ID=4662

CoreNet Global & Deloitte. *Real estate & facilities (RE&F) function in M&A and divestiture activity.* https://resources.corenetglobal.org/knowledgecenteronline/SearchByTopicAndResource.aspx?ID=3793

CPA Journal. *Capitalizing lease payments.* https://resources.corenetglobal.org/knowledgecenteronline/SearchByTopicAndResource.aspx?ID=3467

Deloitte. (2010). *Lease administration benchmarking survey.* https://resources.corenetglobal.org/knowledgecenteronline/SearchByTopicAndResource.aspx?ID=6447

Ernst & Young. *Corporate transactions: opportunities abound, but proceed cautiously.* https://resources.corenetglobal.org/knowledgecenteronline/SearchByTopicAndResource.aspx?ID=572

Ernst & Young. *Good real estate (international) limited: International GAAP illustrative financial statements.* https://resources.corenetglobal.org/knowledgecenteronline/SearchByTopicAndResource.aspx?ID=3099

Newmark Grubb Knight Frank. (2014, February). *12 changes likely affecting commercial real estate in 2014.* http://www.naiop.org/en/E-Library/Business-Trends/Twelve-Changes-Likely-to-Affect-CRE-in-2014.aspx.

Chapter 6

CoreNet Global. Corporate real estate fundamentals. Part 2: CRE finance. https://resources.corenetglobal.org/knowledgecenteronline/SearchByTopicAndResource.aspx?ID=4640

CoreNet Global. *Real estate: Cost centre or profit enhancer?* https://resources.corenetglobal.org/knowledgecenteronline/SearchByTopicAndResource.aspx?ID=5401

CoreNet Global & CBRE. *Capital planning: Measuring the return on capital for office facilities projects' webinar.* [Presentation]. https://resources.corenetglobal.org/knowledgecenteronline/SearchByTopicAndResource.aspx?ID=1002

Jones Lang LaSalle & VFA. *How to forecast and manage capital spend.* https://resources.corenetglobal.org/knowledgecenteronline/SearchByTopicAndResource.aspx?ID=3953

Nelson. *Driving down cost through workplace strategies: Installment 1. The physical space.* https://resources.corenetglobal.org/knowledgecenteronline/SearchByTopicAndResource.aspx?ID=5435

Nelson. *Driving down cost through workplace strategies: Installment 2. Amount of space.* https://resources.corenetglobal.org/knowledgecenteronline/SearchByTopicAndResource.aspx?ID=5162

Newmark Grubb Knight Frank. *The Influence of Capital Markets on Corporate Real Estate.* https://resources.corenetglobal.org/knowledgecenteronline/SearchByTopicAndResource.aspx?ID=5996

Newmark Grubb Knight Frank. *12 changes likely affecting commercial real estate in 2014.* https://resources.corenetglobal.org/knowledgecenteronline/SearchByTopicAndResource.aspx?ID=4013

Chapter 7

Cushman & Wakefield. (2012–2013). *Global trends in real estate outsourcing.* https://resources.corenetglobal.org/knowledgecenteronline/SearchByTopicAndResource.aspx?ID=3674

Kaplan, B., Newgreen, A. (2014). *Changing the conversation from cost to value: Optimizing the integrator model—three years on.* Report from CoreNet Global Asia Pacific Summit. https://resources.corenetglobal.org/knowledgecenteronline/SearchByTopicAndResource.aspx?ID=4268

KPMG. (2013). *2013 global real estate & facilities management (REFM) outsourcing pulse survey.* https://resources.corenetglobal.org/knowledgecenteronline/SearchByTopicAndResource.aspx?ID=4380

Risks and rewards. How to optimize complex multi-provider outsourcing strategies. (2010). Report from CoreNet Global Summit, Phoenix. https://resources.corenetglobal.org/knowledgecenteronline/SearchByTopicAndResource.aspx?ID=566

Chapter 8

CB Richard Ellis. *Evaluating your critical facilities.* https://resources.corenetglobal.org/knowledgecenteronline/SearchByTopicAndResource.aspx?ID=6411

CoreNet Global. *Proactive asset management: Integrating facilities management with business priorities.* https://resources.corenetglobal.org/knowledgecenteronline/SearchByTopicAndResource.aspx?ID=3745

CoreNet Global. *The CoreNet Global facilities management survey.* https://resources.corenetglobal.org/knowledgecenteronline/SearchByTopicAndResource.aspx?ID=6597

CoreNet Global. *Workplace experience levels: Putting the human equation back into global facilities management.* https://resources.corenetglobal.org/knowledgecenteronline/SearchByTopicAndResource.aspx?ID=5731

Chapter 9

CoreNet Global & Deloitte. (2012). Corporate real estate performance management. *Research Bulletin.* https://resources.corenetglobal.org/knowledgecenteronline/SearchByTopicAndResource.aspx?ID=2956

CoreNet Global & DTZ. *Corporate real estate benchmarking techniques.* https://resources.corenetglobal.org/knowledgecenteronline/SearchByTopicAndResource.aspx?ID=6194

CoreNet Global & Newmark Grubb Knight Frank. *Technology: Reporting and analytics' webinar.* [Presentation]. https://resources.corenetglobal.org/knowledgecenteronline/SearchByTopicAndResource.aspx?ID=538

CoreNet Global. *Building the bridge: Positioning corporate real estate for the new corporate metrics.* https://resources.corenetglobal.org/knowledgecenteronline/SearchByTopicAndResource.aspx?ID=1542

Corney, G., & Jervis, M. (2010, September/October). Performance measurement: Know your position, realize your value, and move forward. *The Leader,* pp. 12–16. https://resources.corenetglobal.org/knowledgecenteronline/SearchByTopicAndResource.aspx?ID=4301

Georgia Institute of Technology. *Benchmarking of the building performance toolkit for GSA.* https://resources.corenetglobal.org/knowledgecenteronline/SearchByTopicAndResource.aspx?ID=5481

Jones Lang LaSalle. *Perspectives on occupancy strategy.* https://resources.corenetglobal.org/knowledgecenteronline/SearchByTopicAndResource.aspx?ID=6599

KPMG. (2012). Using a balanced scorecard to help measure facilities management performance. *Shared Services and Outsourcing Advisory,* 1–4. https://resources.corenetglobal.org/knowledgecenteronline/SearchByTopicAndResource.aspx?ID=2203

Music, D., Nager, A., & Tucker A. (2011, September/October). Corporate real estate best practices: A methodology to effectively benchmark performance. *The Leader,* pp. 40-44. https://resources.corenetglobal.org/knowledgecenteronline/SearchByTopicAndResource.aspx?ID=6210

Chapter 10

Anderson, M., Acoba, F., Dobson, C., & Davidson, C. (2010). *Integrated workplace management systems: The management of real estate and facilities management information technology platforms.* Report from CoreNet Global Research & Deloitte Consulting.

Badgett, M., Ellerthorpe, R., & Swanstrom, M. (2012). *Corporate real estate 2020, technology tools: Final report.* Atlanta, GA: CoreNet Global.

CoreNet Global & Deloitte Consulting. *Integrated workplace management systems.* https://resources.corenetglobal.org/knowledgecenteronline/SearchByTopicAndResource.aspx?ID=4813

CoreNet Global. *Extreme integration: Managing real estate information for maximum impact.* https://resources.corenetglobal.org/knowledgecenteronline/SearchByTopicAndResource.aspx?ID=4158

CoreNet Global. *Maximizing the value of new technology in today's CRE management.* https://resources.corenetglobal.org/knowledgecenteronline/SearchByTopicAndResource.aspx?ID=4091

CoreNet Global. *Positive impact: How new IWMS developments are improving the bottom line.* https://resources.corenetglobal.org/knowledgecenteronline/SearchByTopicAndResource.aspx?ID=6503

CoreNet Global. *Technology problem solution: New business intelligence tools accelerate reporting and analytics.* https://resources.corenetglobal.org/knowledgecenteronline/SearchByTopicAndResource.aspx?ID=2378

Dow Chemical. *From concept to execution: How to make IWMS a reality.* https://resources.corenetglobal.org/knowledgecenteronline/SearchByTopicAndResource.aspx?ID=4044

Drake, C., & Tackett, P. (2014). Taking your physical space inventory to the next level. *Report from FM Strategies, Little's Space Management and Facility Planning Studio.*

IWMS. *A practical approach for real estate professionals.* https://resources.corenetglobal.org/knowledgecenteronline/SearchByTopicAndResource.aspx?ID=6311

Sprint & CBRE. *Portfolio risk information system (PRISM).* https://resources.corenetglobal.org/knowledgecenteronline/SearchByTopicAndResource.aspx?ID=6734

Chapter 11

Borce, M. (2014). *Practical project management in real estate development.* http://mebibo.com/practical-project-management-in-real-estate-development/

CoreNet Global & CBRE. *Next-generation PMO's: A key to enhancing strategic partnerships.* https://resources.corenetglobal.org/knowledgecenteronline/SearchByTopicAndResource.aspx?ID=1728

CoreNet Global. (2011). *Transforming Chevron's CBRES into a 21st century services organization.* Breakout session at Atlanta Summit. https://resources.corenetglobal.org/knowledgecenteronline/SearchByTopicAndResource.aspx?ID=4935

CoreNet Global. *A great transaction doesn't ensure great occupancy . . . unless project management is part of the process.* https://resources.corenetglobal.org/knowledgecenteronline/SearchByTopicAndResource.aspx?ID=1077

CoreNet Global. *Gensler's Shanghai tower.* https://resources.corenetglobal.org/knowledge-centeronline/SearchByTopicAndResource.aspx?ID=1729

CoreNet Global. *Reducing waste and increasing value through corporate energy management: Johnson Controls.* https://resources.corenetglobal.org/knowledgecenteronline/SearchByTopicAndResource.aspx?ID=6230

EC Harris. *Feasibility studies: The asset test.* https://resources.corenetglobal.org/knowledge-centeronline/SearchByTopicAndResource.aspx?ID=6354

Chapter 12

CoreNet Global. *Advocacy statement: Energy management and conservation.* https://resources.corenetglobal.org/knowledgecenteronline/SearchByTopicAndResource.aspx?ID=4152

CoreNet Global. *Corporate occupier sustainability study.* https://resources.corenetglobal.org/knowledgecenteronline/SearchByTopicAndResource.aspx?ID=6788

CoreNet Global. *Improving the sustainability and value of buildings.* https://resources.corenetglobal.org/knowledgecenteronline/SearchByTopicAndResource.aspx?ID=3767

CoreNet Global. *Reducing waste and increasing value through corporate energy management: Johnson Controls.* https://resources.corenetglobal.org/knowledgecenteronline/SearchByTopicAndResource.aspx?ID=6230

CoreNet Global. *Setting your sustainability ambitions.* https://resources.corenetglobal.org/knowledgecenteronline/SearchByTopicAndResource.aspx?ID=2187

CoreNet Global. *The Leader special whitepaper: Sustainability beyond green buildings.* https://resources.corenetglobal.org/knowledgecenteronline/SearchByTopicAndResource.aspx?ID=1306

DTZ. *What Price Compliance? The Fridge Factor.* https://resources.corenetglobal.org/knowledgecenteronline/SearchByTopicAndResource.aspx?ID=6446

Jones Lang LaSalle. *Global sustainability perspective: Green buildings and office worker productivity.* https://resources.corenetglobal.org/knowledgecenteronline/SearchByTopicAndResource.aspx?ID=5222

Chapter 13

Allsteel. *NetWork: The future workplace.* https://resources.corenetglobal.org/knowledgecenteronline/SearchByTopicAndResource.aspx?ID=6713

Bugg, A., Scroggie, P., & Tucker, A., & Newmark Knight Frank Global. *Portfolio: Drive productivity . . . and reduce cost!* https://resources.corenetglobal.org/knowledgecenteronline/SearchByTopicAndResource.aspx?ID=2060

Cisco Iomerics. (2013). *Workplace design transformed by research and big data.* https://resources.corenetglobal.org/knowledgecenteronline/SearchByTopicAndResource.aspx?ID=6209

CoreNet Global & Newmark Knight Frank. *Productivity metrics survey results.* https://resources.corenetglobal.org/knowledgecenteronline/SearchByTopicAndResource.aspx?ID=768

CoreNet Global. *Alternative workplace strategies: Building the business case.* https://resources.corenetglobal.org/knowledgecenteronline/SearchByTopicAndResource.aspx?ID=3275

CoreNet Global. *Alternative workplace strategy: What's really working? A global benchmarking study.* https://resources.corenetglobal.org/knowledgecenteronline/SearchByTopicAndResource.aspx?ID=4126

CoreNet Global. *Corporate real estate 2020 final report: Workplace.* https://resources.corenetglobal.org/knowledgecenteronline/SearchByTopicAndResource.aspx?ID=4423

CoreNet Global. *Flexible workspace: Before, during and after change.* https://resources.corenetglobal.org/knowledgecenteronline/SearchByTopicAndResource.aspx?ID=5888

CoreNet Global. *Moving beyond alternative workplace strategy: After 20 years can AWS finally scale-up?* https://resources.corenetglobal.org/knowledgecenteronline/SearchByTopicAndResource.aspx?ID=3963

CoreNet Global. *The living office.* https://resources.corenetglobal.org/knowledgecenteronline/SearchByTopicAndResource.aspx?ID=1247

CoreNet Global. *Well-being in the workplace.* https://resources.corenetglobal.org/knowledgecenteronline/SearchByTopicAndResource.aspx?ID=5068

CoreNet Global. *Workplace: Shifting work styles are creating shifts in where we work.* https://resources.corenetglobal.org/knowledgecenteronline/SearchByTopicAndResource.aspx?ID=3101

EC Harris. *Corporate real estate: Increase productivity.* https://resources.corenetglobal.org/knowledgecenteronline/SearchByTopicAndResource.aspx?ID=4693

Steelcase. *360 Deepdive: How emerging work strategies are changing the workplace.* https://resources.corenetglobal.org/knowledgecenteronline/SearchByTopicAndResource.aspx?ID=3143

Chapter 14

CoreNet Global. *Be prepared for change: Business continuity trends and considerations.* https://resources.corenetglobal.org/knowledgecenteronline/SearchByTopicAndResource.aspx?ID=3985

CoreNet Global. *Business impact of Hurricane Sandy: Flexibility becomes mission-critical.* https://resources.corenetglobal.org/knowledgecenteronline/SearchByTopicAndResource.aspx?ID=2042

CoreNet Global. *Supporting employee flexibility and business continuity at Monsanto.* https://resources.corenetglobal.org/knowledgecenteronline/SearchByTopicAndResource.aspx?ID=2446

CoreNet Global. *The business impact of Superstorm Sandy.* https://resources.corenetglobal.org/knowledgecenteronline/SearchByTopicAndResource.aspx?ID=1761

CoreNet Global. *The evolution of business continuity and risk management: What are the implications for corporate occupiers?* https://resources.corenetglobal.org/knowledgecenteronline/SearchByTopicAndResource.aspx?ID=3163

Jones Lang LaSalle. *Preparing for a pandemic: Strategies for business continuity when a crisis hits home.* https://resources.corenetglobal.org/knowledgecenteronline/SearchByTopicAndResource.aspx?ID=5456

Jones Lang LaSalle. *Surviving the disaster zone: Lessons learned in Asia Pacific.* https://resources.corenetglobal.org/knowledgecenteronline/SearchByTopicAndResource.aspx?ID=3027

Chapter 15

CoreNet Global. *Corporate real estate 2020 final report: Partnering with key support functions.* https://resources.corenetglobal.org/knowledgecenteronline/SearchByTopicAndResource.aspx?ID=3449

CoreNet Global. *Corporate real estate 2020 final report: Partnering with key support functions (webinar).* https://resources.corenetglobal.org/knowledgecenteronline/SearchByTopicAndResource.aspx?ID=518

CoreNet Global. (2012, September/October). Partnering with key support functions: the importance of integrated resource models. *The Leader,* pp. 30-34. https://resources.corenetglobal.org/knowledgecenteronline/SearchByTopicAndResource.aspx?ID=5293

Dobrian, J. (2014, September/October). Polycom, Inc.: Partnering for enterprise success. *The Leader,* p. 51. https://resources.corenetglobal.org/knowledgecenteronline/SearchByTopicAndResource.aspx?ID=2510

CoreNet Global & Newmark Grubb Knight Frank. *"HR, CRE, IT & Finance Partners in Strategy": Survey results.* https://resources.corenetglobal.org/knowledgecenteronline/SearchByTopicAndResource.aspx?ID=2501

CoreNet Global & Newmark Grubb Knight Frank. *"HR, CRE, IT & Finance Partners in Strategy": Webinar.* https://resources.corenetglobal.org/knowledgecenteronline/SearchByTopicAndResource.aspx?ID=6079

Chapter 16

Arkesteijn, M. H., & Heywood, C. (2013, September). *Enhancing the alignment process between CRE & organisational strategy.* Presentation at CoreNet Global Summit, Amsterdam. https://resources.corenetglobal.org/knowledgecenteronline/SearchByTopicAndResource.aspx?ID=3646

CoreNet Global. *Corporate real estate 2020 final report: Enterprise leadership.* https://resources.corenetglobal.org/knowledgecenteronline/SearchByTopicAndResource.aspx?ID=532

CoreNet Global. *Real estate professionals vs. business professional? Corporate real estate's role in influencing business strategy.* https://resources.corenetglobal.org/knowledgecenteronline/SearchByTopicAndResource.aspx?ID=1926

Johnson Controls & CoreNet Global. *Change management survey results presentation.* https://resources.corenetglobal.org/knowledgecenteronline/SearchByTopicAndResource.aspx?ID=5976

Microsoft Corporation. (n.d.) *Evolution of workplace at Microsoft.* PowerPoint presentation, Redmond, WA.

Shaner, C. (2012, May). *Corporate real estate 2020: Enterprise leadership final report.* Atlanta, GA: CoreNet Global.

Silen, S. (2012). *Real estate strategy alignment: Getting it right.* Houston, TX: KPMG. https://resources.corenetglobal.org/knowledgecenteronline/SearchByTopicAndResource.aspx?ID=4416 KPMG

Chapter 17

Allsteel. *NetWork: The Future Workplace.* https://resources.corenetglobal.org/knowledgecenteronline/SearchByTopicAndResource.aspx?ID=6713

Colliers. *Generation Y: Space planning and the future of workplace design.* https://resources.corenetglobal.org/knowledgecenteronline/SearchByTopicAndResource.aspx?ID=3250

CoreNet Global. *Corporate real estate: A future view.* https://resources.corenetglobal.org/knowledgecenteronline/SearchByTopicAndResource.aspx?ID=5811

CoreNet Global. *Flexible workplace: The future of the workplace.* https://resources.corenetglobal.org/knowledgecenteronline/SearchByTopicAndResource.aspx?ID=4993

CoreNet Global. *How business is changing: A framework for the year 2020.* https://resources.corenetglobal.org/knowledgecenteronline/SearchByTopicAndResource.aspx?ID=748

CoreNet Global. *The Future of CRE Technology.* https://resources.corenetglobal.org/knowledgecenteronline/SearchByTopicAndResource.aspx?ID=5315

CoreNet Global. *The future of globalization.* https://resources.corenetglobal.org/knowledgecenteronline/SearchByTopicAndResource.aspx?ID=1532

Heerwagen, J., Anderson, D., & Porter, W. (2012). *Network: the future workplace.* Cambridge, MA: Anderson Porter Design.

Jones Lang LaSalle. (2003). Jones Lang LaSalle selected by P&G for $700 million facilities management contract. [Press release]. http://www.prnewswire.com/news-releases/jones-lang-lasalle-selected-by-pg-for-700-million-facilities-management-contract-71196667.html.

Palomba, D. (2013) *Corporate real estate industry future trends and keys to successful outsourcing.* [PowerPoint presentation]. http://www.slideshare.net/DickPalomba/corenet-presentation-5–16–2013-corporate real estate-trends-and-keys-to-successful-outsourcing-513

Pereira, M. (2013, March/April). The future of CRE technology. *The Leader.* https://resources.corenetglobal.org/knowledgecenteronline/SearchByTopicAndResource.aspx?ID=5315

Procter & Gamble. (n.d.). *P&G's Global Business Services.* [Brochure]. Cincinnati, OH.

Shehadi, R., & Karam, D. (2014, January). *Five essential elements of the digital workplace: Strategy+business.* http://www.strategy-business.com/blog/Five-Essential-Elements-of-the-Digital-Workplace?gko=eebed

Stack, T. (2013, March). *Shift happens 2013: The world of work.* [PowerPoint Presentation]. CoreNet Global Summit, Shanghai, China. https://resources.corenetglobal.org/knowledgecenteronline/SearchByTopicAndResource.aspx?ID=1481

Telefonica. *The world in 2020.* https://resources.corenetglobal.org/knowledgecenteronline/SearchByTopicAndResource.aspx?ID=3616

Index